Forms of Organising in Industrial History

This shortform book presents key peer-reviewed research selected by expert series editors and contextualised by new analysis from each author on different forms of organising British industry.

With contributions on the strengths and weaknesses of the holding company structure, government organisation of industry during war time, the effects of forms of organisation on innovation, and debates over the suitability of international comparisons, this volume provides an array of fascinating insights into industrial history.

Of interest to business and economic historians, this shortform book also provides analysis and illustrative case-studies that will be valuable reading across the social sciences.

John F. Wilson is Pro Vice-Chancellor (Business and Law) at Northumbria University, Newcastle. He has published widely in the fields of business, management, and industrial history, including ten monographs, six edited collections, and over seventy articles and chapters.

Steven Toms is Professor of Accounting at the University of Leeds. He is a former editor of Business History. His research interests are focused on accounting and financial history and the history of the textile industry.

Ian G. Jones is a Senior Research Assistant at Newcastle Business School, Northumbria University, and won the John F. Mee Best Paper Award at the Academy of Management in 2018 for his contribution to the Management History Division.

Routledge Focus on Industrial History
Series Editors: **John F. Wilson, Steven Toms** and **Ian G. Jones**

This shortform series presents key peer-reviewed research originally published in the *Journal of Industrial History*, selected by expert series editors and contextualised by new analysis from each author on how the specific field addressed has evolved.

Of interest to business historians, economic historians and social scientists interested in the development of key industries, the series makes theoretical and conceptual contributions to the field, as well as providing a plethora of empirical, illustrative and detailed case studies of industrial developments in Britain, the United States and other international settings.

A Search for Competitive Advantage
Case Studies in Industrial History
Edited by John F. Wilson, Steven Toms and Ian Jones

Knowledge Management
Dependency, Creation and Loss in Industrial History
Edited by John F. Wilson, Ian Jones and Steven Toms

The Development of Professional Management
Training, Consultancy, and Management Theory in Industrial History
Edited by John F. Wilson, Ian Jones and Steven Toms

Forms of Organising in Industrial History
Edited by John F. Wilson, Steven Toms and Ian G. Jones

For more information about this series, please visit: www.routledge.com/Routledge-Focus-on-Industrial-History/book-series/RFIH

Forms of Organising in Industrial History

**Edited by John F. Wilson,
Steven Toms and Ian G. Jones**

Routledge
Taylor & Francis Group

LONDON AND NEW YORK

First published 2022
by Routledge
4 Park Square, Milton Park, Abingdon, Oxon OX14 4RN

and by Routledge
605 Third Avenue, New York, NY 10158

Routledge is an imprint of the Taylor & Francis Group, an informa business

© 2022 selection and editorial matter, John F. Wilson, Steven Toms and Ian G. Jones; individual chapters, the contributors

British Library Cataloguing-in-Publication Data
A catalogue record for this book is available from the British Library

Library of Congress Cataloging-in-Publication Data
Names: Wilson, John F., 1955- editor. | Toms, Steven, editor. |
Jones, Ian G., 1987- editor.
Title: Forms of organising in industrial history/edited by John
F. Wilson, Steven Toms and Ian G. Jones.
Description: Abingdon, Oxon; New York, NY: Routledge, 2022. |
Series: Routledge focus on industrial history |
Includes bibliographical references and index.
Identifiers: LCCN 2022009208 (print) | LCCN 2022009209 (ebook) |
ISBN 9781032322117 (hardback) | ISBN 9781032322124 (paperback) |
ISBN 9781003313397 (ebook)
Subjects: LCSH: Industrial organization–Great Britain–History. |
Holding companies–Great Britain–History. |
Industrial management–Great Britain–History.
Classification: LCC HD70.G7 F675 2022 (print) | LCC HD70.G7 (ebook) |
DDC 338.0941–dc23/eng/20220301

LC record available at https://lccn.loc.gov/2022009208
LC ebook record available at https://lccn.loc.gov/2022009209

ISBN: 978-1-032-32211-7 (hbk)
ISBN: 978-1-032-32212-4 (pbk)
ISBN: 978-1-003-31339-7 (ebk)

DOI: 10.4324/9781003313397

Typeset in Times New Roman
by Deanta Global Publishing Services, Chennai, India

Contents

Contributors

Robert Fitzgerald – Robert Fitzgerald is currently a Professor at Royal Holloway, University of London. He has published on a wide variety of topics including employment relations, marketing, business organisation, economic development, the Asia Pacific economies, and multinational business. His most recent book is *Rise of the Global Company: Multinational Enterprise and the Making of the Modern World.*

John Quail - John Quail received his external doctorate in business history from Leeds University in 1996. He has never held an academic post, not for the want of trying but applications for first academic posts when you are the same age as the head of department will never go very well. He has contributed to a number of business history journals and edited compilations. In retirement he has been appointed a Visiting Fellow in York Management School.

John Singleton – John Singleton is Professor of Economic and Business History at Sheffield Hallam University having previously worked for Victoria University in New Zealand. He has published extensively on various topics, including international trade with New Zealand, central banking, the British textile industry, and the British mining industry. He has published eight books, the most recent being *Economic and Natural Disasters Since 1900: A Comparative History*.

Introduction

Purpose and significance of the series

The concept of the *Routledge Focus on Industrial History* series was motivated by the desire of the editors to provide an outlet for articles originally published in the defunct *Journal of Industrial History* (*JIH*). By using an extensive repository of top-quality publications, the series will ensure that the authors' findings contribute to recent debates in the field of management and industrial history. Indeed, the articles contained in these volumes will appeal to a wide audience, including business historians, economic historians and social scientists interested in longitudinal studies of the development of key industries and themes. Moreover, the series will provide fresh insight into how the academic field has developed over the past 20 years.

The editors believe that the quality of scholarship evident in the articles originally published in the *JIH* now deserve a much broader audience. The peer-reviewed articles are built on robust business-historical research methodologies and are subject to extensive primary research. The series will make important theoretical and conceptual contributions to the field and provide a plethora of empirical, illustrative and detailed case studies of industrial developments in the United Kingdom, the United States and other international settings. The collection will be of interest to a broad stratum of social scientists, especially business school and history department academics, because it provides valuable material that can be used in both teaching and research.

Building on the original Journal of Industrial History

The first edition of the *Journal of Industrial History* was published in 1998, with the aim of providing 'clear definitional parameters for industrial historians' and in turn establishing links between 'industrial history

DOI: 10.4324/9781003313397-1

and theoretical work in social science disciplines like economics, management (including international business), political science, sociology, and anthropology'. Because it has been more than 20 years since its original publication, it is clear that the relevance of the *JIH* has stood the test of time. The original *JIH* volumes covered a diverse range of topics, including industrial structure and behaviour, especially in manufacturing and services; industrial and business case studies; business strategy and structure; nationalisation and privatisation; globalisation and competitive advantage; business culture and industrial development; education, training and human resources; industrial relations and its institutions; the relationship between financial institutions and industry; industrial politics, including the formulation and impact of industrial and commercial policy; and industry and technology. The current *Routledge Focus on Industrial History* series will provide a cross-section of articles that cover a wide range of themes and topics, many of which remain central to management studies. These include separate volumes: *Management and Industry*; *Banking and Finance*; and *Growth and Decline of American Industry*. The *Routledge Focus on Industrial History* series will reframe highly original material that illustrates a wide variety of themes in management and organisation studies, including entrepreneurship, strategy, family business, trust, networks and international business, focusing on topics such as the growth of the firm, crisis management, governance, management and leadership.

Volume Ten

The first chapter, 'The competitive and institutional advantages of holding companies: British business in the inter-war period' by Robert Fitzgerald, argues that the holding company organisational structure, common in Britain in the inter-war period, could be a source of competitive advantage rather than a weakness as is commonly argued. Fitzgerald uses the examples of the textile industry and the armaments industry where the holding company structure provided an advantage as it allowed firms to diversify and benefit from size and scope. Fitzgerald then compares these organisational structures to Japanese and German firms, arguing that the holding company structure may have been suited to British, German, and Japanese markets where scale production was less beneficial.

Fitzgerald's article sparked a response from John Quail, which is reproduced in Chapter Two, which Fitzgerald, in turn, responded to, reproduced in Chapter Three. Quail argues against Fitzgerald's conclusions, stating that although holding companies could provide potential benefits and advantages to firms, in practice, they rarely did, with the reasons for this being unclear. Quail also argues against the comparison to Japanese firms, stating that comparisons are unsuitable due to the origin of Japanese holding companies, their intentions, and forces that held them together. Fitzgerald counters these points and builds on his original article, calling for more research to better understand the history of British management. These chapters present a valuable historiographical debate on interpretations of British management and organisational structures in the twentieth century that show the development of new ideas and reinterpretation of historical sources.

The fourth chapter, 'The tank producers: British mechanical engineering in the Great War' by John Singleton, returns the focus to British industry and the network of factories that were involved in tank production during World War One. Singleton shows the problems associated with tank production, such as the competing demands for resources and skilled labour needed to produce other armaments and the loss of skilled workers, such as draughtsmen, to conscription before they were exempted. This chapter shows that, contrary to common interpretations, British engineers were capable of innovative problem solving as well as collaboration with each other and knowledge sharing between firms to overcome difficulties. However, this collaboration required the British government to intervene to organise their efforts and remove the competitive pressures of external markets; once the British government ceased to do this at the end of the war, few firms continued to work collaboratively, this form of organisation broke down, and the new skills and experiences gained during the war were not utilised as it was difficult to find commercial applications for the wartime technologies.

Conclusion

It is apparent from this brief review of the chapter that the tenth volume in the series makes important contributions to the field of industrial history in several ways. Firstly, it provides a series of high calibre and unique studies in aspects of industrial history that contribute to more recent debates on forms of organising industry, the role of government in directing organisation, and strengths and weaknesses of common forms of organisation. Secondly, the chapters shed light on the broader subjects of sources of the suitability of comparing industries in different nations, differing sources of competitive advantage within a national context, and raises questions about whether market forces bolster or inhibit innovation. Finally, this volume provides strong historical case-studies that can be used by students and researchers who are exploring issues related to forms of organising industry in Britain. The editors believe that this volume will not only provide a much wider audience for articles that link into a range of topical issues but also feed into debates in the wider social sciences. These are themes that will be demonstrated in previous volumes in the *Routledge Series of Industrial History*, highlighting the intrinsic value in republishing material from the *Journal of Industrial History* and ensuring that the articles contribute extensively to current debates.

1 Debates and Speculations

The Competitive and Institutional Advantages of Holding Companies: British Businesses in the Inter-War Period

Robert Fitzgerald

1. British Business and Holding Companies

Are we any nearer, after decades of research and debate, to a settled judgement on the failings of British business organisation and management? Recent work – reassessing the European experience – appears more cautious than certain, raising questions about the conclusiveness of available evidence. Amongst the many areas of contention, family firms and their presumed weaknesses have received particular attention, and revisionism might usefully be applied to several corporate types. Other issues have also caused controversy: the comparative performance of British industry, the suitability of U.S. corporate structures to other nations, and the almost-exclusive emphasis on systems internal to the firm have all been cited. Interestingly, holding companies encapsulated these disputed points: they developed in Britain during a period of relative economic decline; they differed in important respects to the hierarchical managerial enterprise; and they facilitated external linkages between companies, arguably at the cost of inward dimensions. They have, therefore, been prominent targets of a sustained and powerful critique, in which the deficiencies of large-scale companies are portrayed as compounding the economic difficulties of inter-war Britain. From this perspective, many concerns located in the staple industries could not fully adapt to changes in international and domestic demand, because loosely co-ordinated structures and a weak strategic, headquarters function hindered schemes of rationalisation. British holding companies of the 1920s and 1930s have been reproached as the worst examples of such weaknesses, because inadequate central direction and integration enabled uncompetitive constituent firms and detrimental family-control to continue. As a group, they are seen as handicapped in comparison to international competitors and to the rising model of integrated,

DOI: 10.4324/9781003313397-2

managerial enterprise; in other words, their assumed lack of professional personnel, organisational hierarchy, and formal procedures were inappropriate to the challenges of modern industry.[1] Other judgements have been less condemnatory, because some of their early structural and administrative failings were quickly corrected. Further re-assessment of the empirical evidence might review the reputation of the British holding company. On matters of interpretation, the 'rationality' of any managerial structure has been linked to varying economic, financial, or legal circumstances. The universal applicability of a single model is consequently in doubt.[2] We might ask if holding companies offered commercial and operational advantages, despite their being associated – often justifiably – with institutional sclerosis and vested interests.

Is it possible, then, to list alongside known deficiencies the appropriateness of British business organisation in general and the holding company in particular? Because holding companies are frequently viewed as an imperfect form of big business, or as an inchoate form of managerial enterprise, the benefits are rarely stated. One difficulty is the lack of detailed, especially archival evidence at the level of individual firms, despite some wellknown exceptions.[3] A satisfactory response would admittedly require a book as herculean in its endeavour as Chandler's *Scale and Scope*. In the meantime, a re-examination of corporate structures in major industries – in which holding companies were prominent – may provide preliminary insight into future research questions. Clearly, the law in Britain was more permissive of alliances and groups than the U.S., but competitive and institutional advantages may also have encouraged or maintained the holding company form in particular sectors. The most fitting structure for any concern depends on multiple factors, and the requirements of product markets, production processes, and the fluctuating economic fortunes of the inter-war years might all be reconciled with the holding company. Financial systems, moreover, should be noted. International comparisons are needed to clarify the appropriateness of managerial forms to their circumstances, as well as the relative contribution of corporate governance to the success or failure of companies and whole industries. But, before looking at the commercial or operational aptness of large-scale organisation in the British shipbuilding and textile industries, the characteristics of the holding company and current debates on managerial enterprise should be re-stated.

2. Holding Company Structures

In attempting to understand the organisational forms adopted by British business, the term 'holding company' may act as a barrier to understanding, because its use conceals a broad spectrum of arrangements in governance and operations. Holding companies have been linked in British business history to the maintenance of family control and the existence of business groups or alliances, although neither association is automatic. In essence, they describe a main company with a controlling interest in or authority over legally separate and mainline subsidiaries, which are given responsibility for production or operations. In some cases, this arrangement might have formalised existing private or family-based holdings; in other cases, it might be the result of newly-merged interests or acquisitions; or, alternatively, an attempt to liberate the management of distinct units which were once more integrated or supervised. Where the ownership of constituent firms is reposed within a parent company, a number of variations in organisational characteristics may result. At one extreme, those directly associated with member businesses may retain voting control, and prefer to maintain separate operations and administrative functions. This internal settlement may be very similar to a business group or alliance, or even to a price-fixing arrangement, despite the formal pooling of interests within a main company. Such arrangements were typical of British mergers in textiles, tobacco, and building materials at the turn of the century.[4] Yet the link between firms is permanent rather than merely opportunistic, as in the case of business alliances, and creates the possibility of further organisational developments. As a result, many of the early large-scale companies in the textile industry were subsequently restructured. The headquarters function of holdings companies is, indeed, too frequently viewed as permanently weak, just as the span of operations is seen as highly diversified or even unrelated.[5]

At another extreme, therefore, strategy and some core functions such as accounting, marketing, or research may be centralised at the parent firm of holding companies. Such measures were important to the development of several British firms, facilitating the financial and commercial aspects of business, while leaving production in the hands of subsidiaries. In some cases, even personnel policy was harmonised. The multidivisional structure or the M-form, it has been argued, can allocate resources to product divisions in response to performance and market trends, and enable economies of scale in support services. Despite having legally-separate, mainline subsidiaries within specific national boundaries,[6] rather than more integrated divisions, one type of holding company may not differ greatly from the M-form. Japanese cases seem to suggest this convergence in definition and practice,[7] whereas British examples were, it has been assumed, intrinsically deficient or undeveloped in their structures. In theory, neither the headquarters of the 'classic' multidivisional enterprise nor the parent firm in holding companies would assume direct control of operations. The fact that ICI, Britain's best-known inter-war example of an M-form business, seems to have breached this general rule demonstrates the difficulties of terminology and the varied nature of historical experience.[8] Multiple directorships and particular personalities may have initially increased the influence of parent firms within holding companies, but in many cases systems did emerge. The textile firm of J. & P. Coats is known for its organisational awareness, and, by the 1920s, its structure was noticeably 'hybrid': it had the defined product and geographical divisions of the M-form, yet they oversaw the type of subsidiaries associated with holding companies.[9]

As in the case of other governance systems, variations in the form and practice of holding companies undoubtedly complicate definition and assessment. Nonetheless, legally-separate, mainline subsidiaries cannot be accommodated within the U-form and are not traditionally associated with the M-form. Identifiable satellite businesses vested in or controlled by a single privately-owned or incorporated organisation, moreover, excludes short-term alliances, joint ventures, market-fixing trusts and cartels. Collaborative links formed through banks or merely personal ties are clearly not holding companies; nor are groups based on mutual shareholdings between equals, as their grouping differs from an arrangement of parent and subsidiary. Granovetter regards holding companies as only a 'marginal case' to the more general issue of business groups,[10] but this seems an expeditious judgement on their attributes and historical significance. Although holding companies may act as alliances or groups, ownership linkages make holding companies more easily identifiable and their commercial and strategic aims potentially more coherent. Firms join alliances or groups to further their own objectives, and inter-firm co-operation is in consequence conditional. The solidity of the Japanese business groups, or *kigyo shudan*, stems from past ownership links, and, in the immediate post-war years, mutual shareholding and the main bank system were used to secure managerial control within each member enterprise, intentionally excluding external influences. Institutional connectivity in Japan remains an important national characteristic, but it would be a mistake to perceive the group as more important than the constituent companies. Depending on variations in authority structures and managerial resources, holding companies may have specific economic or strategic aims, and even organisational or corporate purposes that are not present in business groups or cartels. It is worth asking if they can demonstrate 'positive' as well as collusive tendencies.

Some commentators prefer to distinguish between 'conglomerates', in which the links between firms are purely financial, and 'groups', where the ties are also personal and operational.[11] Certainly, contrasts in the financial and operational objectives of holding companies have been significant, and, whatever the terminology, the distinction is a useful one in the British context. Speculative booms and merger mania can be found as early as the

1920s, and undoubtedly influenced opinion on stock market promoters and the growing scale of industrial organisation.[12] Debates on 'stakeholding' and on the economic benefits of mergers and acquisitions have formed a recent critique of post-war capitalism in the U.S. and Britain, and holding companies have been viewed as some of the worst examples of short-termism. There are, in addition, associations with off-shore tax avoidance. In their policies towards subsidiaries, several diversified conglomerates from the 1970s infamously relied upon financially-orientated targets and asset-stripping.[13] The holding company form was suited to the acquisition and easy sale of companies, although it was post-war changes in the stock market and industrial ownership which accentuated these trends. Yet short-termism is not inherent to one form of industrial organisation, and national failings in business finance, human capital, and technology have complicated and multidimensional explanations.[14] The symptoms of short-termism can be found in a range of large-scale British companies.

Any interpretation of organisational aptness is by necessity case-specific and contingent, and, as the history of Japanese big business demonstrates, change can be anticipated. The original diversified operations held privately by the old *zaibatsu* families often became divisions of an incorporated company or even separate businesses,[15] and, in several instances, these were subsequently transformed into holding companies with a main concern and dependent subsidiaries. In the post-war years, when holding companies were illegal, they re-emerged as groups more loosely connected by history, banks, chief executives' meetings, or mutual share transfers. Holdings companies have, too, a noticeable place in the history of British capitalism, emerging at the turn of the century, and becoming more prominent during the inter-war period. Two prominent cases were the British shipbuilding and armaments industry and the textile sector. Their holding companies have been depicted as monopolistic in intent, inhibiting industrial rationalisation and the evolution of managerial efficiencies. The detail of their governance structures in fact demonstrates no evident pattern, but case-studies do show instances of reorganisation that were responses to commercial and administrative requirements. Ships and armaments were capital goods dependent upon infrequent orders and batch production methods, and textiles, with more limited manufacturing returns to scale, could gain from the co-ordination of purchasing and marketing. In the years following the First World War, therefore, rapid expansion, diversification, and vertical coordination between separately-managed enterprises became objectives. Within these industries, product, production and market requirements encouraged or maintained the holding company organisation rather than the 'classic', integrated structure in furtherance of these corporate aims.

3. Organisation, Integrated Enterprise and the Business Environment

The criticisms of British big business and its holding companies in the inter-war period have emerged from our growing understanding of managerial enterprise. The successful businesses described by Chandler contain an organisational hierarchy, which is capped by a headquarters responsible for strategy, and underpinned by divisional and then departmental levels overseeing operations. Together, these layers of management compose and govern an incorporated, unitary enterprise, and this particular system of corporate co-ordination and control is associated with mass production and the successful exploitation of scale and scope economies.[16] Chandler employs transaction cost analysis to explain why a vertically-integrated and unified firm possessed advantages over the market as a mechanism for gathering information and processing goods. U.S. manufacturing companies gained from mass production by internalising transactions, as new hierarchical administrative structures exerted a centralised control over functional departments and then product divisions. By peering inwards and towards the efficiency properties of internal systems, Chandler did not expand upon international variations in the nature of markets and exchanges, nor upon intermediate mechanisms between firms and markets such as business networks, inter-company links, and industry-finance relationships. In understanding the connectivity between individuals and institutions, regional and national factors are important, and so too are industry-specific influences.[17]

Boyce, in his intriguing investigation of the British shipping industry before the First World War, uses principal-agent theory to demonstrate the relevance of inter-firm communication and operating links. He distinguishes between the need for hierarchical, integrated structures in manufacturing and the different imperatives of the service sector. Large industrial concerns had to maintain and utilise the loyalty and expertise of managers through administrative structures, because they were employed for their specialised knowledge of tangible products and processes, in which returns to scale became prominent. Shipowners, on the other hand, relied on contacts and on the commercial intelligence of agents, and they made client or trade-specific investments in vessels. They harnessed these connections through the reciprocity, reputation and repeat contracting of business networks, which in addition enabled the raising or pooling of capital whenever required. The absence of vertical integration was not an indicator of competitive decline but reflected the product market and operational realities of the shipping industry. In short, the concept of the entrepreneur as organisation-builder differs from that of the entrepreneur as deal-maker. Large shipping firms did emerge – often adopting the holding company form – and they possessed enhanced capabilities in the gathering of information and finance. There was generally no shift towards a central hierarchy, because the subsidiaries retained the commercial intelligence, contract-making capabilities, and other intangible assets, and because they inter-acted infrequently.[18] The distinction between industry and trade appears valid, but seems to accept the failure of British manufacturing organisation.[19] Yet product markets and operational processes varied even between industrial concerns, and in certain cases they have encouraged or reinforced business networks and holding companies.

Few would dispute the importance Chandler attaches to the development of large-scale business and the emergence of managerial personnel and systems in twentieth century industry. Like his suspicion of family involvement, his preference for a specific ownership and organisational structure is more questionable. Regional clusters and networks of small and medium-sized firms have been portrayed as alternatives to big business,[20] and they are linked too with products, production systems and markets in which the benefits of standardised production, deep organisational hierarchies, and a large corporate head-quarters were not so readily available.[21] To be exact, Chandler himself acknowledges the contingent technological and demand factors that favoured large-scale enterprise within certain sectors, largely those identified with the 'second industrial revolution'.[22] Nonetheless, the concept of 'best practice' for large manufacturers has been authoritative, and the perceived utility of managerial enterprise has tended to disregard the advantages of family firms, business groups, alliances, and holding companies. As has been argued elsewhere, the continuation of controlling family interests within large companies did not necessarily hinder the creation of administrative hierarchies, so that the dichotomy of family control versus the advantages of professionalisation appears fallacious.[23] Some authors, moreover, have noted the economic rationale of business groups and alliances, their examples often drawn from Japan, but additionally from Germany,[24] and inter-firm co-operation has been interpreted as an apposite response to the market inefficiencies of 'late development'.[25]

Chandler states that he has written an 'internal history of the central institution in managerial capitalism', and his large-scale modern enterprise is 'managed by a hierarchy of full-time salaried executives' who compose an integrating governance function capable of co-ordinating 'a number of distinct operating units'. Big business is seemingly measured by this particular administrative yardstick, which the federated ownership and operational structures of even the better-managed British holding companies did not possess. Overall, Chandler's powerful thesis points to a general failure in Britain's large-scale companies. *Scale and Scope* extended his previous seminal works on U.S. business structures into international comparison, in a search for the underlying causes of national competitiveness. He uncovers 'common patterns of institutional growth' within leading countries, and investigates the implications.[26] Through this approach, he emphasises the internal characteristics of firms, and the U.S. emerges in effect as the model for other industrial nations to follow. Unsurprisingly, such a bold analysis was subjected to close scrutiny, and some commentators were unconvinced by the attempt to identify distinctive national characteristics in big business organisation. Tools used in the analysis of individual concerns were not so successfully applied to whole economies.[27] Britain as the bastion of 'personal capitalism' – in which family management, amateurism, a lack of managerial hierarchy, and weak holding company structures are especially noticeable – seems too great a generalisation or characterisation.

In a re-examination of big business, its history, and stages of development, we might alternatively weigh both the benefits and weaknesses of managerial enterprises, family involvement, holding companies, or group alliances, according to differing economic, historical and institutional circumstances. In attempting to evaluate any 'common patterns of institutional growth', the U.S. might instead be seen as a special case, one well-suited by the inter-war period to managerial enterprise, and as consequentially different to Germany, Japan and Britain. A fuller account of national business environments is therefore necessary. Combination was prohibited in the U.S. under the Sherman Act, and a huge domestic market maximised company scale and organic growth at specific production stages. With abundant natural resources minimising concern over the security of supplies, vertical as well as horizontal co-operation between firms was limited. Within the large, integrated enterprises that emerged, the span of administrative control and capital demands assisted the professionalisation of management and ownership changes at the expense of business dynasties.[28] Yet, personal and family influence in U.S. big business continued, and stands as a warning against over-generalisation.[29] Although British corporate culture is adversely depicted as 'personal capitalism', many quoted cases might be evaluated differently. Business strategies, technological change, and distribution systems are covered in detail in many instances, but the evaluation of specific company organisations – a vital variable in the debate – too often depends on evidence that is far from conclusive. In many instances, our knowledge of big businesses and their internal organisation remains thin.[30] From a comparative perspective, Chandler readily contrasts British and German business in the 1920s and 1930s according to the supposed poles of family control versus professionalisation, when the similarities may be more apparent. He acknowledges the importance of alliances and cartel arrangements in Germany, although managerial enterprise has been connected with co-ordination through a single, administrative hierarchy. The rationale and impact of business networks is not analysed in depth, but, seemingly, they did not inhibit the professionalisation of German management. In addition to family involvement and alliances, holding company structures in large-scale business cannot have been innately detrimental, after all, even in the case of Britain.

There are interesting parallels between German industrial organisation and Japanese business structures, which have been described as 'alliance capitalism'.[31] Here, the capabilities of single firms are acknowledged, but the focus shifts to the benefits of co-operative institutional relationships. The business groups of the Japanese have been viewed positively, just as banking and cartel arrangements did not hinder German economic development. A number of influential works have outlined the development of big business in Japan,[32] and, despite much support for Chandler's general thesis, their conclusions and evidence also sustain more widely-based explanations and frameworks.[33] In his overview of a highly informative collection of studies, Chandler concentrates on Japan's establishment of 'hierarchical organisations to co-ordinate their various activities',[34] rather than on examples of family involvement, business groups, and holding companies, in which headquarters control over the operations of separate concerns was neither strong nor consistent.[35] Indeed, a business system of subsidiaries linked through ownership has been seen as important to the circumstances of late industrialisation, technology transfer, and rapid development in key sectors. Operational control was given to the management of subsidiary firms which were associated to a parent concern, its bank or trading company, and Fruin describes this arrangement as one of 'networks and focal factories'.[36]

According to Chandler's description of the modern corporate enterprise, organisational imperatives should be propelled by strategic plans executed through a deep managerial hierarchy that is extended throughout an integrated enterprise. It is a feature of late or rapid development, as witnessed in the case of Japan, that capital and managerial resources were in short supply, and that they were frequently available for new ventures only through government or business groups. Individual firms and plants, urgently evolving systems and adapting new technologies, tended to lessen the number of production-stages under their control, and in effect substituted internalised returns-to-scale for the scope economies and reduced transaction costs of inter-firm connections. In the inter-war period, Japanese big business did not correspond with all of Chandler's specifications, but did share similarities with British holding companies. The vertical links and cartel arrangements of German industry have been similarly described: more limited competition enabled U.S. technology to be applied with lower levels of domestic demand, and supported the building of company-level competencies and production-line efficiencies.[37] The horizontal connections of the larger, older *zaibatsu* in Japan have received particular attention, but vertical, Konzern-type relationships did exist between groups' members and their suppliers and distributors. They were, furthermore, central to the operations of the new *zaibatsu* that emerged in the inter-war period. In other words, differing national circumstances in Germany and Japan moved the advantages away from the managerial enterprise in comparison to the United States. Were there factors, then, which encouraged holding company structures or alternatives to the managerial enterprise within British big business?

4. The Shipbuilding and Armaments Industry

The British shipbuilding and armaments industry of the inter-war period is often and not unreasonably paraded as an example of failure. Explanations are not so apparent, as the diversity of business organisation and international comparison reveal. The firm of Beardmore has become well-known for the commercial difficulties which were to challenge its existence and for the ineffectiveness of its managerial response in the 1920s. It cannot be criticised as unwilling to invest and build modern facilities; this is not a case of enterprise conservatism, but arguably one of incautious risk-taking. Beardmore began the construction of its Dalmuir shipyard, near Glasgow, in 1900, and, when it ran out of credit, it was compelled to bring in the Sheffield firm of Vickers, Son & Maxim, as it was then called.[38] The new site was well-equipped and designed on a grand scale, in the main to meet orders from the Royal Navy, and it allowed the assembly of whole ships, from hulls to fixtures and ordnance. Dalmuir also had the largest fitting-out basin in the world. While building these marine engineering facilities, Beardmore diversified further: it opportunistically bought shares in Masons Gas Power Company, and, in a move intended to assist expansion, it secured supplies through the purchase of the Mossend steel works.[39] Vickers, which on paper had a controlling interest, was worried by the growth and expenditure plans, and attempted to impose restraints. By the end of the First World War, William Beardmore, Lord Invernairn had forced through expansion via subsidiaries into aircraft manufacture, locomotives, steam and oil-powered engines, buses, lorries, taxis, motor-cycles, automobiles, and steel, as well as mining and quarrying.[40]

The post-war boom and declining military orders justified Beardmore's acquisition of subsidiaries and its diversification in products. But the economic circumstances of the 1920s soon left it over-capitalised and unprofitable, even compared to local rivals,[41] and the well-documented sequence of events that beset the company took place during 1926–29. Vickers sold its interest, and, when the Treasury used its leverage under the Trade Facility Acts to change the management, Invernairn himself was ousted.[42] If the personal capitalism prevalent at Beardmore did not demonstrate a lack of entrepreneurship or investment, the owner's autocratic, unbending style was reportedly unsuited to the new challenges of the 1920s. The company was unable to achieve adequate throughput in its subsidiaries, and it began to suffer from an earlier policy of diversification that had once seemed appropriate. As an armaments manufacturer, Beardmore had been faced with the cessation of hostilities, and been presented with the opportunities of the post-war boom. The firm formed a number of vertical and horizontal corporate links, and these offered potential advantages to shipbuilders. The unpredictable and uneven nature of their industry favoured diversification into related or even unrelated products, and the creation of forward and backward networks facilitated supplies in good times and sales orders when conditions were bad. Group structures and holding companies potentially bestowed economies of scope, secured markets, assisted control over materials and costs, dispersed risks, and enhanced financial stability.[43]

Specific charges have been levelled at Beardmore: that managerial resources were inadequate for a firm of its size and diversity, and that, as well as the chairman having no personal office, there was no headquarters function. The main company did have a managing director, a secretariat, and an accounting section by the 1920s, however unsophisticated these may be judged.[44] In any case, weak central control may be a characteristic of specific holding companies, because co-operative institutional links and effective plant-level management can act as the vital organisational capabilities. Whether Beardmore had appropriate levels of managers and technicians within its operational units is an open question, for which there is little documentary evidence. Slaven characterises shipbuilding firms on the Clyde as possessing estimating and costing departments, and a works department or a number of production departments. In 1899, the Sheffield firm of John Brown bought the Clydebank shipyard, near Glasgow, and, before the First World War, it was organised functionally with nineteen departments, and, below them, the engine works alone had sixteen separate units. Qualified people included draughtsmen, naval architects, and engineers, and line management came under the departmental heads, some of whom were appointed to the main board. Thomas Bell, a major figure in the company, was appointed managing director at Clydebank in 1909, and held the post for twenty-six years.[45] In a final assembly process such as shipbuilding, flow and co-ordination at the level of individual plants was a major task for management. Therefore, 'Operating and tactical decisions required to implement policy were clearly delegated to departmental heads...', and below them in the yards were hierarchies of supervisors and workers. Like Beardmore at Dalmuir, John Brown at Clydebank became the shipbuilding section of a horizontally-diverse but vertically-integrated industrial empire.[46]

Beardmore's decline and financial pressures undoubtedly stirred personal tensions and a bitter battle for control,[47] damaging the main company and relations with and between subsidiaries.[48] The dismissal of Invernairn was drawn out, and his removal from the boards of minor companies was even more complex and difficult.[49] Low demand and a lack of throughput seriously weakened several of these subsidiaries, and the uncompetitive prices they quoted as suppliers to associated firms disrupted agreements and mutual relations within the group.[50] When the Bank of England and other interested parties appointed Hans Reincke as chairman in February 1930, he summed up nearly a decade of failings by pointing to the old guard's lack of foresight, poor management, and failure to rationalise.[51] Subsequent reforms were based on a general reorganisation of Glasgow shipbuilding and the reinforcement of management within the Parkhead steel forge and other subsidiaries.[52] Under Reincke, the functions and purposes of all linked firms and major manufacturing investments were investigated and stated; departments overseeing operations such as Locomotives or Commercial Vehicles did exist, and were administered by designated managers; and revitalisation plans were devised for each department.[53] Beardmore's internal problems and failures in the 1920s cannot be denied, but whether they were solely or mainly the result of personalised management or a particular corporate structure is hard to determine. Other factors may have been more important, and there is no easy resolution of the balance between managerial failings and general conditions, such as domestic demand and the role of the state. Comparisons with Japan suggest that it was not the holding company by itself that was problematic, although Beardmore may have become a bad example of its kind. The firm's failings should also be placed in context: it achieved earlier successful growth under the leadership of its founder; the logic and strength of its diversification were recognised and copied; and ultimately new management did systemise Beardmore's very personal style.

Vickers was intimately connected with the history of Beardmore, and had its origins in steel and armaments, finally engaged in naval engineering, and emerged as one of Britain's largest conglomerates. It shared Beardmore's strategy of manufacturing everything needed for a warship, consequently moving into many forms of ordnance, and it anticipated the military use of motorised vehicles by buying car-maker Wolseley. Vickers was one of Britain's most active multinationals in the years before the First World War, establishing overseas plants which could meet the orders of host governments. In the immediate period after 1918, its operations in Britain included locomotives; boilers; turbines; engines of all kinds; machinery and machines tools; gas meters; furniture; and toys; in addition to ships, ordnance, and cars. It also acquired train-lighting, refrigerator, and electric cable companies, and then both Metropolitan Carriage & Wagon and British Westinghouse, which were merged into Metropolitan-Vickers.[54]

The conglomerate was troubled by the same economic conditions and low throughput prevalent in so much of British heavy industry during the 1920s, although its financial affairs under the guidance of the increasingly-bizarre Sir Vincent Caillard may have been a contributory element.[55] Chandler agrees that the company had a well-established tradition of hiring experienced and talented executives and technicians, whilst remaining a family firm. In the restructuring of 1925, subsidiary boards were founded to co-ordinate the three major activities of armaments and shipbuilding, other industrial products, and finance, and, over the next three years, the firm underwent a period of disinvestment.[56] Able, non-family managers were recruited to take control from the family, and Vickers emerged as a profitable and financially-strong company, despite the difficulties of its previous ventures. The company fails to concord with suggested British stereotypes, and relied on interlocking managerial skills and a cabinet-style governance, as opposed to the flair of any individual.[57] In October 1927, it was merged to form Vickers-Armstrong, through which it could bolster the weaker Armstrong Whitworth, and gain from the rationalisation of armaments manufacture.[58] Gauging the depth and quality of Vickers' management at plant-level remains as difficult as other cases, but Chandler presents British Westinghouse, an acquired subsidiary, as a benchmark by which to judge British companies in the inter-war years. One account is critical of the original U.S. management.[59] As always, Britain offers mixed evidence. Before the Great War, Armstrong Whitworth stands in contrast to Vickers. It had seemingly been weakened by an autocratic management style, until administrative reforms modelled on its rival were introduced in 1911. Unrelated diversification into hydroelectricity and Canadian pulp and paper milling further complicated the difficulties confronting its traditional steel and engineering businesses in the 1920s.[60]

From the turn of the century to the years following the First World War, British steel, shipbuilding and armaments manufacturers tended to found diversified conglomerates, firstly in response to growing naval and military expenditure, and subsequently in an effort to secure wartime profit levels during peacetime commerce. At first, links between firms were based on trust relationships and repeat orders, and may have extended to mutual board members and share exchanges. They could facilitate joint ventures and projects, the use of technology and labour, and negotiations with government; ultimately, they might lead to mergers and rationalisation, whilst securing supplies and smoothing the volatile nature of demand. The Clydebank shipyard operated within the John Brown combine, but existed also in a wider network. Before 1914, the group undertook cooperative ventures with Cammell Laird, Fairfield, Vickers, and Armstrong Whitworth, and it cultivated independent and joint contacts at the Admiralty. Whatever the weaknesses of the headquarters function, John Brown's fortunes, institutional relationships, and reputation were all inextricably linked, and the soundness of the Clydebank management was quoted as a source of strength.[61] The Scottish shipbuilders, Lithgow, moved into steelmaking during the 1920s, and extended its engineering interests, finally buying Fairfield, a competitor, in 1935. Fairfield was, in turn, connected to the Anchor Line, which provided links with the maritime transport industry.[62]

In the case of the Furness combine in north east England, however, it was a shipowner who gradually acquired the Palmer shipbuilding facilities, as well as a steelmaker, coalmines, and even a marine insurance business. Ellerman bought William Gray, and Holt purchased Scotts and Caledonia Shipbuilding.[63] Another parallel to the close relationships of Japanese shipping, shipbuilding, and metal manufacturing firms was Lord Inchcape's Peninsular and Oriental line, which acquired the Glasgow yard of Alexander Stephen and the Steel Company of Scotland just after the First World War. It is fair to add that Stephen's link with a major customer hardly sustained adequate throughput in the subsequent, depressed decade. Only one third of its capacity was utilised, but it is hard to see how its commonplace troubles could have been deflected.[64] Harland & Wolff, with its well-connected chairman Lord Pirrie, established connections with Lithgow and the marine engineering company of Weir,[65] and also became part of the Royal Mail Shipping Group in 1918.[66] It has been said that the expertise and focus of the Harland & Wolff management were located at the level of the plant, and again this should be viewed as a strength, not as an automatic deficiency.[67] Colville, a family-owned but professionally managed enterprise, emerged as a formative influence in the restructuring of the Scottish steel industry. By 1920, it was wholly owned by Harland and Wolff, yet it was under the direction of the well-respected Sir John Craig, a career manager.[68] In 1930, it acquired a competitor, John Dunlop & Co., from Sir James Lithgow and his brother, Henry, who then both joined the Colville board, and the shipbuilding firm later used its position as a major customer to merge the Steel Company of Scotland and the Lanarkshire Steel Company with Colville.[69] The reconstruction of the Royal Mail Group between 1931–36 is quoted as an example of a committed relationship between industry and financial institutions. Executives at the Midland Bank provided substantial credit, and were deeply involved in business strategy and rationalisation plans.[70] Sir James Lithgow, moreover, had been a leading figure in the reorganisation of Beardmore in the late 1920s, and his appointments as its director and finally as chairman were merely further confirmation of his pivotal role in the business world of Glasgow.[71]

The interdependency of the shipbuilding, steel, engineering, and shipping industries is apparent, and the co-operative relations encouraged by the Board of Trade committee on shipping and shipbuilding in 1918 became deeper and more complex. Yards with reliable, mutually-advantageous contacts could reduce contracting, design and building costs.[72] Shipbuilders similarly benefited from their links with steel and engineering suppliers, and networks could pool finance and resources in response to big orders. The risk of large-scale capital projects were reduced through personal and inter-firm connections, and their effectiveness and the expertise of works management forestalled vertical integration. Trust, reciprocity and co-operation encouraged repeat contracts, and the reputation of particular individuals and firms often became central to a network. These links were sometimes formalised within holding companies, in an attempt to protect supplies or markets, and, by the late 1920s and the 1930s, certain firms and individuals proved instrumental to the rationalisation of these groups.

Payne, surveying the rise of large-scale business in Britain and the persistence of family control, wonders if some of their difficulties might have been avoided, if they had adopted some variant of the multidivisional structure described by Chandler. He is certainly critical of their 'unjustified belief in the continued efficiency of the holding-company form'.[73] Looking to a wider picture, he states that our understanding of economic growth and industrialisation rests on an evaluation of the all-prevalent family firm. He speculates whether large companies which retained influential dynasties might have inhibited economic growth,[74] an early and perceptive statement of a now powerful case.[75] In terms of furthering new businesses and products, British holding companies in the shipbuilding and engineering sector during the 1920s were ambitious. For their reluctance in developing the heavy and chemicals industries of Japan, the old *zaibatsu* of the inter-war period have ironically been described as 'conservative'.[76] Furthermore, several British heavy industries companies did encourage professional managers, and their influence undoubtedly grew in the 1930s, after wide-scale reorganisation and restructuring within the sector.[77] Tariff protection, rearmament and subsidies no doubt cushioned many enterprises, sometimes limiting or halting new investment or the building of integrated works, but moderate success stories and even exemplars can be found.[78]

5. Management and the Textile Industry

The sudden decline in markets and problems of rationalisation and management were 'much the same', says Chandler, in British textiles as they were in shipbuilding and steel.[79] In horizontally unifying one-time competitors, the British textile combines differed from their compatriot shipbuilding and armaments manufacturers and from the *zaibatsu*, which were more diversified and more vertically inter-connected. It has been noted – not unfairly – that some of the federations which were created at the turn of the century were collusive in intent and lacking in internal dynamism.[80] Early judgements were harsh: the majority of multi-firm mergers were seen as failing to produce any fundamental internal and organisational changes.[81] Confusion seems to have infused policy-making and central administration at the Bleachers Association, and its board of directors seemingly imitated an assembly devoid of any unified purpose.[82] As Chandler is highly critical of British corporate structures and the holding company in particular, he contends that their legal consolidation did not in general promote administrative co-ordination, investment, or managerial recruitment, despite instances of joint purchasing, research, accounting procedures, and overseas transplants. He acknowledges that the Bleachers Association, Calico Printers Association, Bradford Dyers, J. & P. Coats, and the Linen Thread Company all enlarged 'their small corporate offices' in the inter-war years, but blames them for leaving constituent firms in charge of purchasing, processing and sales. In integrating spinning with weaving, and in founding marketing networks, Whitworth & Mitchell, Joshua Hoyle, and Horrocks, Crewdson are quoted as exceptional.[83] Chandler admits that the potential returns to scale in natural fibre manufacturing were not extensive, but looks for vertical integration and co-ordination between production-stages as a means of increasing throughput and lowering costs. On the other hand, as he states, mergers followed by rationalisation were not used to found successful textile enterprises in either the U.S. or Germany.[84] Were British firms, nonetheless, slow in unifying the manufacture of yarn and cloth? Did this greatly affect the competitiveness of the cotton textile industry, or were there counterbalancing efficiencies in regional clustering, efficient market mechanisms, and international trading networks? Its smaller scale, family businesses did not necessarily gain from firm-specific marketing channels. Marshall and Chapman famously described Lancashire as an industrial district, pointing to the varied nature of textile markets, and posing networks as a replacement for vertical integration and scale.[85] Later authors found the long-term failings of the region's cotton companies to be located in its atomistic structure,[86] and the issue remains a contentious debate.[87] But we can more easily ask if the combines that did emerge in

British textiles gained the benefits of vertical integration and co-ordination between production-stages.

The Linen Thread Company was founded between 1898–1900, and eventually linked six British and Irish firms and their U.S. subsidiaries. At the main holding company, board committees were formed to supervise sales, finance, or manufacturing, and a variety of departments were established to oversee selling, bookkeeping, commercial information, invoicing and other functions. There was an early intention to systematise gradually any activity that might benefit from centralisation, although the combine was wary of 'drastic changes' that could cause greater disorganisation. In 1898, the several sales offices inherited from the constituent companies were rationalised, and, when sales staff were placed under the control of the new Glasgow headquarters, resistance was encountered. As a result, it was decided to consider 'steps to secure, without further loss of time, the advantages which the formation of the Linen Thread Company Ltd was intended to secure'. In order to improve the co-ordination of national and international sales and invoicing, member firms were ordered to bring their books to the central office, and a Statistical and Information Department was founded. Although individual factory managers continued to arrange their own purchasing, they were not allowed to hold more than six months of stock without the prior permission of the central Manufacturing Committee. The headquarters determined the remuneration of salaried mill staff, and output was rationalised to a small extent by the closure of the Springburn Mill in Ireland in 1899. As a holding company, LTC was managed through a mixture of decentralised production and centralised support functions, and this structure remained in force during the inter-war years.[88] Additional, if not conclusive evidence, suggests that early changes at Calico Printers Association, Bradford Dyers Association, English Sewing Cotton, and Tootal, Broadhurst and Lee addressed significant managerial issues, although Chandler would view these developments as ultimately insufficient.[89]

Payne believes that another large, merged company, J. & P. Coats, evolved a 'highly efficient bureaucratic structure', and its board oversaw the central direction of statistical information, buying, selling, and accounting. Coats is an example of British success, and, ignorant of the strictures against personal capitalism, it fused family ownership with professionalised management.[90] The firm was converted into a limited company in 1890, the same year in which its marketing branch, the Central Agency, was founded. Five years later, Coats bought up its main rivals in Scotland and England, and owned mills in the U.S., Canada and Russia. With seventeen production units, 150 selling depots, and 21,000 employees across the globe, it was one of Britain's largest companies. Its reputation for efficiency and competitiveness made it a formative influence on the structure and organisation of the textile combines which were established around 1900. Chandler acknowledges the achievements of its international joint sales agency, and the fact that, like the Fine Cotton Spinners and Doublers Association, it recruited non-family managers.[91] Coats was a cotton thread manufacturer, located in Paisley, near Glasgow, which under the chairmanship of Archibald Coats and his sales director, Ernst Philippi, built a worldwide reputation. The expansion of Coats was followed by the merger of fifteen other cotton, linen and silk threadmakers in 1897–99 to form the English Sewing Cotton Company, which was in turn linked to the American Thread Company. Coats was quick to invest in ESCC, and, in the early 1900s, it seconded Philippi to implement much-needed managerial reforms. Within ESCC, the continued involvement of men from the constituent firms was recognised as a mistake, and some mills were rationalised. Its sales organisation was placed within the Central Agency, which in turn gained from enhanced market power and throughput.[92]

The linking of Coats, ESCC and American Thread created a powerful alliance within the international cotton thread industry, although disputes did arise between the parties concerned. Coats, moreover, secured its raw materials of cotton yarn by owning shares in the Fine Cotton Spinners and Doublers Association, and purchased a coalmine that provided energy supplies. FCSDA, founded in 1898, united some thirty-one Lancashire cotton firms, and followed the usual pattern of centralising buying, selling and distribution functions. Executive power seems to have rested with the headquarters, which decided prices and allocated orders. The production mills retained their original identity, and their names were seen as carrying reputation and customer confidence.[93] Coats also held shares in the Calico Printers Association, where Philippi served as chairman of its Reconstruction Committee, introducing effective reforms out of initial organisational chaos, and finally being appointed a director. The use of managerial expertise from Horrockses, Crewdson and the Bleachers Association, as well as Coats, was illustrative of the importance of inter-firm links.[94] Interestingly, when the Linen Thread Company was formed, it also sought advice from Coats and Philippi on matters of managerial organisation. As well as arranging a loan, Philippi supported the centralisation of administrative and selling activities, and LTC's sales department was consequently modelled on the Central Agency. Coats, moreover, appointed a board member to LTC.[95] From its inception, Philippi's famed marketing subsidiary effectively replaced informal price and market share agreements between firms, and it acted to maintain the relative position of its constituent producers through an efficient, integrated, and rationalised selling system. In gaining the even and enhanced throughput of vertical co-ordination, Coats and ESCC bolstered and facilitated the position of the production units and their managers within their respective holding companies.[96] Institutional links with linen thread companies, cotton manufacturers and calico finishers enabled the diversification of investments, but served in addition as a means of exchanging commercial and organisational information. Particular individuals – prominently Phillipi – were at the heart of an effective network of textile executives and owners.

Coats' continued interest in managerial structure, during the inter-war period, has received less attention than its earlier innovations. By the 1920s, Coats had a number of operating Divisions, each supervised by an Executive Committee, and numerous Sub-Committees of the board oversaw matters such as cotton buying, training, welfare, capital expenditure, and advertising. In 1930, it was investigating the position and role of the subsidiaries, and it was intent also on 'important internal changes in the organisation of the parent Company'. The overall aim of reform was to improve managerial control and general efficiency, by formally deciding on the balance of responsibilities between the Glasgow headquarters and the constituent firms. Whilst central functions such as purchasing, finance, accounting, and technical assistance were to be improved, a holding company structure continued to offer authority and operational freedom to the production units and the Central Agency. Nevertheless, the constitutions of local mill committees were re-drafted to comply with overall objectives, and a Quality Sub-Committee was charged with imposing production and product standards. The mills at Paisley and in England were grouped into a single subsidiary, United Thread Mills Ltd, which formed a new Division alongside the businesses in Vienna, the U.S. companies, the wholly-owned overseas subsidiaries, and associated foreign companies. Their policies were co-ordinated through separate Executive Committees. At Glasgow, a Merchandising Department was formed to consider those issues which fell between production and marketing, since this aspect of product differentiation, packaging and advertising had been poorly done, 'if at all'. The Central Agency was instructed to improve the flow of information on sales estimates, so that manufacturing output could be better planned, and the new Merchandising Department, taking over the central warehouse, allowed the mills to focus on production. Furthermore, Heads of Department were appointed to manage the new functionally-defined central activities. At the Glasgow headquarters, expenditure was ultimately subjected to more detailed scrutiny, and the Cost Section was converted into a separate Department to service both the Finance and the Budget and Costs Sub-Committees.[97]

During the inter-war period, Lancashire's cotton industry did not in the main demonstrate the same capacity for product and organisational innovation as the threadmakers, whose markets were more buoyant and less dependent upon batch production. The integration of spinning and weaving continued to lag behind the rising competitors of Japan, and the dominant smaller scale, family enterprise remained commercially independent.[98] The establishment of the Lancashire Cotton Corporation in 1929 was partly brokered by the Bank of England, and its aim was to rationalise spinning and increase the throughput of medium and coarser yarns. Because the LCC was not universally welcomed, the relationship between the main company and the mills was tense, and it was slow in acquiring and rationalising plant.[99] Legislation and compulsory levies did achieve by the later 1930s considerable progress in the concentration of the industry, but questions about Lancashire's ability to absorb new technology and co-ordinate overseas sales remained.[100] A large and important section of the cotton industry appeared unable to fulfil its organisational requirements, but its experience was not necessarily typical of other large concerns.

Although authors have rightly stressed the role of horizontal merger in the formation of British textile holding companies, acquisition did occur; so, too, did the vertical co-ordination of production and marketing. Overall, some claims of administrative failings and lost synergies appear exaggerated. Support activities such as accounting, finance, purchasing, and sales functions were centralised, when deemed beneficial. The control of production management at the level of mills may be explained by institutional legacy, but was sometimes counterbalanced by the involvement of board committees, divisions or a designated subsidiary. The economies of vertical integration and the limited opportunities for scale returns were additional reasons. In the thread, linen, and fine cotton sectors, British companies proved able to adapt, and gained advantages from the co-ordination of support functions, the centralisation of purchasing and marketing, and from vertical links within and between firms.

6. Holding Companies Compared

Were the organisational solutions of international competitors in the shipbuilding and textile sectors distinct from those of British companies? In fact, parallels in business strategy and structure can be found in Japanese enterprises, even though their success in the inter-war period is often contrasted. It is differences in economic circumstances and in the role of government that seem more determinant. The major *zaibatsu* which came to dominate the Japanese economy and its heavy industry were holding companies, within which managerial practices, authority structures, and levels of family involvement varied. But, generally, it can be said that their headquarters operated only loose control over the many satellite subsidiaries that made up these business groups.[101] As in the case of British shipbuilding, the themes of diversification, batch production, inter-firm connections and works-level management influenced organisational structures. The *zaibatsu* were not predominant in cotton textiles, but scope economies, vertical linkages, and local control were factors which similarly maintained the holding company form.

One important example of business organisation in the Japanese shipbuilding industry is Mistsubishi Goshi Kaisha, established as a public company in 1893. Under these arrangements, the Iwasaki family owned a number of different enterprises, including the marine engineering works at Nagasaki.[102] Operations were originally organised centrally, but what Morikawa calls 'operationally defined divisions' slowly emerged. Shipbuilding was encouraged by naval orders and successive wars, and by government legislation in the 1890s that subsidised long-distance shipping routes and technologically-advanced vessels. A large order from the shipping line, Nippon Yusen Kaisha (NYK),[103] spurred the development of Mitsubishi Nagasaki as Japan's premier, most modern shipyard. Because of the operation's importance, and partly because of dissension with local management, the *zaibatsu*'s top-salaried executive became located at the yard. A major reorganisation in 1908 changed the system of 'operationally defined divisions' into a system of formal 'operating divisions', which implemented their own regulations, accounting procedures, and personnel management, and were able to act in an independent manner. The resultant structure does not quite conform to Chandler's prescriptions, given the weakness of the headquarters function, but there is some correspondence to the notion of decentralised divisions or the M-form. As shipbuilding continued to expand, Mitsubishi established a works at Kobe in 1905 and another at Hikoshima in 1914. Nagasaki and these two facilities evolved before and during the First World War as the development base for power plant, automobiles, heavy equipment, and planes.[104] In coping with such a diversity of products, Mitsubishi Goshi founded a holding company structure, in which the key role of local management was acknowledged. In 1917, it transformed its subsidiaries into public companies, and these were responsible for shipbuilding, iron and steel, banking, and trading. A further subsidiary in automobiles and aircraft was founded in 1920, and, in 1934, it was merged with the shipbuilding interests as Mitsubishi Heavy Industries (MHI).[105] With its extensive interests in banking and trading, the Mitsubishi group differed from the holding companies and networks of British shipbuilding, but organisational structures and principles had much in common.

By different route and timings, Mitsui also came to be based on the holding company form. In 1893, Mitsui organised its diversified enterprises into four unlimited partnerships, and initial structure and subsequent practice recognised the long-established independence of the units. It was Mitsui Bussan, the *zaibatsu*'s general trading company,[106] that acquired a small-scale shipbuilding division, and, through its purchase of Hokkaido Colliery and Steamship, it gained control of steel and iron-making plants. Centrifugal tendencies were accentuated by the greater willingness of the Mitsui family, compared to the Iwasakis, to release control to salaried managers, and the *zaibatsu* developed as a number of somewhat autonomous corporations.[107] In 1909, Mitsui Gomei Kaisha was officially founded as a means of consolidating the operationally-independent subsidiaries, which were changed over the next two years from unlimited partnerships into public concerns. Reformers at the main company had sought to imitate Mitsubishi Goshi, which was at this point controlled more centrally. Yet, by some irony, it was Mitsubishi that in 1917 followed the holding company form established at Mitsui by default.[108] Interestingly, Mitsubishi Shipbuilding (MSC) and Mitsui were the two shipbuilding firms that best weathered the economic travails of the 1920s, and they respectively benefited from close links with NYK and the shipping division of Mitsui Bussan. Kawasaki Shipbuilding had connections with Kawasaki Steamship,[109] and the larger lines of NYK and OSK, but it carried other comparative disadvantages. Its investments, overcommitment in a particular shipbuilding sector, and failure to rationalise hampered its competitive and financial performance. The resources and opportunities of the established *zaibatsu* were undermined in the 1920s by a sharp decline in their major areas of trading, mining, and marine and general engineering.[110] To stimulate a moribund shipbuilding sector, the government began in 1932 to subsidise the scrapping of old vessels and the building of modern ships. It was these policies, as well as military and naval orders, that transformed the Japanese industry and offered adequate throughput, not any major change in the nature or structure of management.[111] British subsidies occurred later and less comprehensively.

Mitsubishi and Mitsui were not unusual. Suzuki states that the holding company became the dominant form in Japan between 1920 and 1930. He also notes the devolution of managerial functions within these enterprises, and he argues that dynamism emerged from the individual firms, not the groups themselves.[112] The managerial and staffing resources available to Mitsubishi Goshi and Mitsui Gomei were small compared to the operational subsidiaries or their plants, where policy as well as production decisions were formulated. In the 1920s, Mitsubishi Shipbuilding employed some 3,000 people in its two shipyards. At both Nagasaki and Kobe, there was a functionally-orientated management not dissimilar to that practised by British contemporaries. The headquarters at Mitsubishi Shipbuilding had two small departments concerned with trading and technology, but there was little co-ordination of production or even sales between the two shipyards. In 1920, the main company had some 80 permanent staff who were paid monthly, but Nagasaki was to employ 1,534 administrative and technical staff, whilst Kobe possessed 853.[113] Militarisation and war-time administration of the economy subsequently instigated direct dealing between government and subsidiary management, and the growing power of the state weakened the co-ordinating role of the main *zaibatsu* or their head offices.[114]

The nature of production and operational scale in the cotton textile industry were less complex than the case of shipbuilding, but, as in Britain, a number of giant concerns did emerge in Japan during the 1920s. Yui notes the prominence of merger activity in this decade,[115] as 40 per cent of the cotton industry came under the control of three companies, Kanegafuchi Spinning, Toyo, and Dai Nippon.[116] Organisational gains were found in the vertical linking of purchasing and sales through group structures, just as the holding company in Britain made these advantages possible. When Kanegafuchi was progressively acquired by Mitsui Bussan, it was granted access to a vast trading network. Within the industry as a whole, there was no widespread effort to place merged interests within single integrated businesses that were strategically controlled by a headquarters function or operational divisions. Historical focus upon the horizontally-diverse *zaibatsu* tends to underplay the crucial relations between the subsidiaries and their component suppliers, in addition to the vertical connections of prominent new *zaibatsu* companies, such as Nissan and Nitchitsu.[117] Similarly, links along the value chain between manufacturing units, suppliers and buyers offered economies of scope, purchasing power, and marketing access to the Japanese cotton textile industry. Despite the mergers of the 1920s, therefore, Suzuki acknowledges the role and relative independence of functionally-orientated management structures within many textile factories, and he notes the smallness of company headquarters. As in the case of the British combines, it proved easier to consolidate commercial activities than the manufacturing units, the result being resistance to centrally-controlled production departments.[118]

There are obvious similarities between the structures and ownership patterns of the Japanese *zaibatsu* and large cotton enterprises and those of the holding companies and groups characteristic of Britain in the 1920s. In both cases, the headquarters function was not considered as important as subsidiary-level management, although, arguably, the *zaibatsu* extracted greater advantages from institutional links between operational units. Chandler states that large-scale U.S. businesses preferred geographical and product diversification through a multidivisional structure, and that a key, strategic role was given to the corporate headquarters. Vertical integration, with the early exception of rubber and oil, was not a chosen means of development. This pre-war pattern in the U.S. can be contrasted with the semblance between Britain and Japan. In Germany, the large-scale merger of Vereinigte Stahlwerke in 1926 did not alter the autonomy of its many subsidiaries, and the structures of Krupp and GHH reflected their preference for both vertical co-ordination and product diversification. The *Konzerne*, it is argued, were frequently family-owned, and could operate with weak central administration or with only the centralisation of supporting services, such as marketing or purchasing.[119] By minimising competition and enhancing trading stability, horizontally-orientated cartels enabled companies to employ U.S. technology with German levels of demand, while financial discipline was maintained by the influential 'Big Banks'. A commitment to vertical links and tied suppliers put an emphasis on production efficiencies at each stage in the value chain. Both of these factors sheltered the evolution of manufacturing plant competencies,[120] in a manner that recalls Fruin's description of Japanese business groups as co-operative alliances and focused factories.[121] Product diversity, vertical connections, and subsidiary-level control of production encouraged many examples of holding companies and business groups in Britain, Japan and Germany. Evidence from Europe and notably Belgium suggests nonetheless, that the holding company was the most suitable means of providing industrial finance and exercising corporate governance.[122]

7. Firms, Linkages and Organisation

The development of business organisation, company size, and the aptness of corporate structures have been interpreted from a number of perspectives. The concept of transaction costs has helped to explain the relationship between firms and markets,[123] but corporate links and inter-firm co-operation are intermediate aspects of business behaviour which have additionally attracted the interest of economists and historians, most obviously with regard to culture and trust relationships.[124] If established links, personal connections and customary practice can substitute for an absence of formal administrative hierarchy, they might operate effectively within federated organisational structures, groups and holding companies. These ideas are concerned, furthermore, with the operation of value-chains and industrial districts that were characteristic of several industries, including textiles. They are also reminiscent of debates about speciality production, which is not solely concerned with small or medium-sized businesses. Due to technical and market diversities, some large-scale companies engaged in mass manufacturing that required continuous production runs and highly capital-intensive processes; others such as shipbuilding and engineering undertook customised or batch orders that necessitated greater flexibility in the organisation of operations and skills. As customised or batch output implies product diversity, local control of the manufacturing process within companies would follow. Certain sectors such as natural textiles demonstrated scope economies while not possessing the same returns to scale, although they also engaged in customised and batch output. In both cases, centrally-controlled production might not be an overriding goal, yet extensive marketing channels, mass purchasing, and the co-ordination of support services could all be captured within holding companies or in forms less integrated than the 'classic' managerial enterprise. Federated structures, weak headquarters supervision of production, and strong plant management are associated with product diversity and scope economies, which were often necessitated by rapid economic growth, risk dispersal, and the search for financial instability in unstable markets. Institutional variety can consequently be anticipated within big companies,[125] and managerial enterprise was neither inevitable nor permanent, but an option for certain industries at particular times.[126]

Within British textiles, mergers at the turn of the century were not always effectively expedited, but, from the evidence available, there were notable, later changes in the governance of these large combines. What occurred was the centralisation of purchasing, marketing, and support activities such as accounting, invoicing and commercial information. As well as having some impact on costs, efficiency, and planning, throughput in an industry where the scale of each production unit was relatively small could consequently be improved. In theory, the skills and flexibility of the British labour force at this time would have further facilitated scope economies, in addition to customisation and the production of high quality goods, although international competitors gradually benefited from new technologies and greater vertical integration. Multisubsidiary and holding company structures secured supplies and markets, and improved contacts with domestic and overseas customers. These advantages were further enhanced by institutional links and alliances between the combines themselves. Parallels with the Japanese cotton industry – the existence of holding company structures and decentralised production management – only reinforce the conclusion that specific organisational characteristics did not weaken Britain, or that other, more important factors must be considered in combination.

While natural textile firms gave priority to scope economies, returns to scale were more easily available in shipbuilding and engineering. Those industries that were capital-intensive and subject to large fluctuations in orders and markets could gain the greatest advantages from business groups and inter-firm connections. Security of supply was needed during good trading conditions, although high material costs were a long-term

danger, and trusted customers were an asset in poor economic circumstances. Shipbuilding, mechanical engineering, steelmaking, ordnance, and
shipping were associated businesses, and upstream and downstream partners
counterbalanced inherent commercial difficulties and assisted fluctuations in
throughput.[127] The infrequency of large capital orders additionally encouraged involvement in less directly-related operations, such as automobiles,
transportation, and electrical engineering, in the hope they could provide
alternative cash-flows. Holding company structures were suited to the maintenance of these linkages and to the supervision of a highly-diversified enterprise. In the years before the Second World War, engineering, shipbuilding
and armaments firms in Britain and Japan both shared holding company
structures. The legal framework in both countries was permissive, and product markets, production requirements and economic circumstances were all
influential. Yet determining the rationality of their organisational choices is
to confront our dearth of detailed information, and at times it delves into an
unprovable assumption about the importance of managerial structures.

Boyce argues that the shipping companies gained from size and scope
economies, rather than scale, and that vertical networks and links were
more critical than integrated managerial hierarchies. Holding companies
maintained the operational independence of subsidiaries and agents – with
their client-specific contacts and skills – and solidified a network of information and finance. In some cases, a committee system achieved a degree
of centralisation and monitoring, and, while some firms invested in management, they did not build deep hierarchies.[128] A re-assessment of the holding
company can be extended to other sectors. One famous but misunderstood
case is the Cadbury-Fry conglomerate, the manufacturer of confectionery,
which was formed in 1918. Its two halves remained nominally independent,
but in practice the Cadbury management was in charge. Separate production
facilities were required by the consumer goodwill invested in their different
brands, and, in the 1920s, purchasing, sales and distribution were quickly
co-ordinated. Cadbury and Fry were effectively joined in 1935, by which
time it was controlled by a structured and professionally-staffed managerial
hierarchy. Its smaller rival, Caley-Mackintosh – created in 1932, and fully
amalgamated in 1939 – were the confectionery industry's 'guilty' party.
While it, too, had to maintain product diversity and brand loyalty, they were
slow to obtain available synergies in the supply and marketing functions.[129]

Further interesting comparisons to shipbuilding, engineering and textiles
can be found in the inter-war public utilities. The formation of holding companies directly linked the gas industry to financial institutions in the city,
and investors were drawn to a business that was capital-intensive but secure
in its profits. In some notable cases, merged interests brought gains in technical services, accounting procedures, marketing, bulk purchase, and new

investment. Given the technological requirements of gas production and distribution, the operational control of local management was nonetheless retained.[130] It seems that holding companies engaged in electricity generation were not viewed positively, although our knowledge of them and their impact is very limited. Accusations of monopolistic pricing were made, but arguments about the need for rationalisation, regulation and a national grid were general to the whole industry.[131] Public utilities and monopolies were marked by a complex system of legislative and ancillary controls, and by a growing pressure to purchase and merge entrenched local concerns, and these political and economic factors shaped the objectives of holding companies in gas and electricity. As we have seen, vertical linkages, product diversity, rapid corporate growth, or risk aversion were goals in the textile, shipbuilding and engineering sectors, although the centralisation of support services combined with the localisation of production management could be found within holding companies overseeing gas supply. Evidence suggests that the power industries were, like the railways, leaders in the development of professionalised, non-family management and corporate organisation, with or without the holding company form. Their size, capital demands, and public ownership all conditioned this early trend within the utilities. Holding companies in large-scale manufacturing reveal greater diversity in their corporate governance: some retained the influence of founding families; some had introduced professional managers; some were merely loosely co-ordinated federations; some had divisional structures; others had strong central staffs.[132]

Finally, organisational parallels between specific industries in Britain, Japan and Germany are apparent. For Japanese big business, alliances were not viewed as responses to market failure,[133] but as a means of supplementing or developing markets through co-operation between companies. In circumstances of 'economic backwardness', rapid growth and industrialisation could outpace the development of markets in finance, human resources, supply networks and distribution, and the intermediation of business groups and holding companies could act as their 'substitutes'. In many countries, including Britain, the size of domestic demand might equally have influenced corporate scale and organisatinal choices. Vertical links and scope economies might have been more important to British, Japanese, and German industries than those in the U.S., where integrated managerial enterprises dealing with more discrete production stages were a more likely outcome. Changes in economic conditions or declining markets, in turn, influenced potential throughput, and affected choices in company size and structures, as did government policies, legal frameworks and financial institutions. These, sometimes contradictory, factors shaped the advantages of the holding company in Britain during the inter-war period. As we have stated, the textile combines formed at the turn of the century were often defensive postures against international competitors, but organisational reforms were soon necessitated. Contracting markets in the inter-war period further accelerated the search for efficiencies; improved monitoring procedures, bulk purchasing and effective marketing channels; and, by the 1930s, co-operation between industry and government brought measures to rationalise overcapacity in the cotton industry. During the post-war boom of 1918–21, the holding company clearly enabled shipbuilding and engineering companies to diversify rapidly into related, non-military products; with the arrival of economic difficulties, vertical linkages and product diversity might have protected sales and cash-flows. As in the textile industry, the long-term contraction of markets eventually forced rationalisation in the late 1920s and throughout the 1930s, and this was achieved within holding company structures. Although it might not have been a major cause of corporate success or failure, it was an organisational form that could be accommodated with specific production processes, products, and markets, and it consequently offered certain companies competitive and institutional advantages. Whether managerial structure – in all its forms – failed British industry is a question that only extensive further research or evidence can resolve. Ultimately, answers may depend on asking other questions. Whether British managers and personnel failed in their stewardship is even more problematical, and we require more information on the nature of decision-making in British companies.

Notes

1   See A. D. Chandler, *Scale and Scope: the Dynamics of Industrial Capitalism* (Cambridge, Mass., 1990); and also W. Lazonick, *Business Organisation and the Myth of the Market Economy* (Cambridge, England, 1991).

2   J. F. Wilson, *British Business History, 1720–1994* (1995), pp. 106–10, 154–5; M. W. Kirby and M. B. Rose, 'Introduction', in *Business Enterprise in Modern Britain* (1994), pp. 17–18. See also L. Hannah, *The Rise of the Corporate Economy* (1983), p. 87.

3   For example, ICI, Unilever, Rowntree, and Cadbury-Fry.

4   Hannah, *Rise of the Corporate Economy*, pp. 8–26; P. L. Payne, 'The Emergence of the Large-scale Company in Great Britain, 1870–1914', *Economic History Review*, vol. 20 (1967), pp. 519–42; M. A. Utton, 'Some Features of the Early Merger Movements in British Manufacturing Industry', *Business History*, vol. 14 (1972). See also H. W. Macrosty, *The Trust Movement in British Industry: A Study of Business Organisation* (London, 1907).

5   See the cases of textiles and the shipbuilding and engineering industry below.

6   Naturally, overseas subsidiaries would have to be incorporated.

7   Note the subsequent discussion of the structures adopted by Mitsubishi and Mitsui in 1908 and 1909 respectively, and the later emergence of legally-separate

subsidiaries from private firms in charge of specific products or industrial sectors. See also Morikawa, *Zaibatsu* (Tokyo, 1992), pp. 1–24, 57–92, 106–14, 126, 128, 130, 145–6, 183, 192.

8 See Hannah, *Rise of the Corporate Economy*, pp. 79–89.

9 See below.

10 M. Granovetter, 'Coase Revisited: Business Groups in the Modern Economy", *Industrial and Corporate Change*, vol. 4 (1995), pp. 93–130.

11 H. Strachan, *Family and Other Business Groups in Economic Development: The Case of Nicaragua* (New York, 1976), p. 20.

12 Hannah, *Rise of the Corporate Economy*, pp. 54–69;

13 G. Jones, 'Great Britain: Big Business, Management, and Competitiveness in the Twentieth-Century Britain', in A. D. Chandler (ed.), *Big Business and the Wealth of Nations* (Cambridge, 1997), esp. pp. 124–7.

14 See B. Elbaum and W. Lazonick, *The Decline of the British Economy* (Oxford, 1985); S. Tolliday, *Business, Banking and Politics: the Case of Steel, 1918–36* (Cambridge, Mass., 1987). For different perspectives, see M. W. Kirby, 'Institutional Rigidities and Economic Decline: Reflections of the British Experience', *Ec.H. R*, vol. xlv (1992), pp. 637–60; S. N. Broadberry and N. F. R. Crafts, 'Britain's Productivity Gap in the 1930s: Some Neglected Factors', *Journal of Economic History*, vol. 52 (1992), pp. 531–58.

15 The shares of the parent companies within the old *zaibatsu* were not listed on the stock exchange during most of the inter-war period, and the founding families remained in control. Pressure from the public and the military later forced concessions. In the new *zaibatu*, such as Nissan and Nichitsu, finance was raised from the stock exchange at an early point in their development.

16 A. D. Chandler, *Strategy and Structure: Chapters in the History of Industrial Enterprise* (Cambridge, Mass., 1962); A. D. Chandler, *The Visible Hand: the Management Revolution in American Business* (Cambridge, Mass., 1977); Chandler, *Scale and Scope*; A. D. Chandler, F. Amatori, and T. Hikino, *Big Business and the Wealth of Nations*; A. D. Chandler and H. Daems (eds), *Managerial Hierarchies: Comparative Perspectives on the Rise of the Modern Industrial Enterprise* (Cambridge, Mass., 1980); A. Chandler, 'The Emergence of Managerial Capitalism', in M. Granovetter and R. Swedberg (eds), *The Sociology of Economic Life* (Boulder, CO, 1992), pp. 131–58; D. F. Channon, *The Strategy and Structure of British Enterprise* (London, 1973); L. Hannah, ed., *Management Strategy and Business Development: an Historical and Comparative Study* (London, 1976); Hannah, *Rise of the Corporate Economy*; C. Schmitz, *The Growth of Big Business in the United States and Western Europe, 1850–1939* (London, 1993).

17 On this point, see H. Kitshelt, 'Industrial Governance Structures, Innovation Structures, and the Case of Japan', *International Organisation*, vol. 45 (1991), pp. 453–93.

18 G. Boyce, *Information, Mediation and Institutional Development: the Rise of the Large-Scale Enterprise in British Shipping, 1870–1914* (Manchester, 1995), pp. 1–10, 291–4.

19 Boyce, *Information, Mediation and Institutional Development*, p. 7.

20 M. Piore and C. Sabel, *The Second Industrial Divide: Possibilities for Prosperity* (New York, 1984); C. Sabel and J. Zeitlin (eds), *Worlds of Possibility: Flexibility and Mass Production in Western Industrialisation* (Cambridge,

England, 1997). See also A. Marshall, *Industry and Trade* (London, 1919); A. Marshall, *The Pure Theory of Domestic Values* (London, 1930).

21 P. Scranton, *Endless Novelty: Speciality Production and American Industrialisation, 1865–1925* (Princeton, 1997); P. Scranton, 'Webs of Productive Association in American Industrialisation: Patterns of Institution-Formation and their Limits, Philadelphia, 1880–1930', *Journal of Industrial History*, vol. 1 (1998), pp. 9–34; G. Tweedale, *Steel City: Enterprises, Strategy and Technology in Sheffield, 1743–1993* (Oxford, 1995).

22 J. P. Hull, 'From Rostow to Chandler to you: How Revolutionary was the Second Industrial Revolution?', *Journal of European Economic History*, vol. 25 (1996), pp. 191–208.

23 R. Church, 'The Family Firm in Industrial Capitalism: International Perspectives on Hypotheses and History', *Business History*, vol. 35 (1993), pp. 1–16; G. Jones and M. B. Rose (eds), *Family Capitalism* (London, 1993); R. Church, 'The Limitations of the Personal Capitalism Paradigm', *Business History Review*, vol. 64 (1990), pp. 703–10; L. Hannah, 'Scale and Scope: Towards a European Visible Hand?', *Business History*, vol. 33 (1991), pp. 297–309.

24 M. Grannovetter, 'Coase Revisited: Business Groups in the Modern Economy', *Industrial and Corporate Change*, vol. 4 (1995), pp. 93–129; P. A. O'Brien, 'Industry Structure as a Competitive Advantage: the History of Japan's Post-War Steel Industry', in C. Harvey and G. Jones (eds), *Organisational Capability and Competitive Advantage* (London, 1992), pp. 128–59; M. Fletcher, 'Co-operation and Competition in the Rise of the Japanese Cotton Industry, 1890–1926', *Asia Pacific Business Review*, vol. 5 (1998), pp. 45–70; W. M. Fruin, *The Japanese Enterprise System: Competitive Strategies and Co-operative Structures* (Oxford, 1994); M. L. Gerlach, *Alliance Capitalism: the Social Organisation of Japanese Business* (Berkeley, CA, 1992); T. Shiba and M. Shimotani (eds), *Beyond the Firm: Business Groups in International and Historical Perspective* (Oxford, 1997).

25 A. Gershenkron, *Economic Backwardness in Historical Perspective* (Cambridge, Mass., 1962); T. Hikino and A. H. Amsden, 'Staying Behind, Stumbling Back, Sneaking Up, Soaring Ahead: Late Industrialisation in Historical Perspective', in W. J. Baumol, R. R. Nelson and E. N. Wolff (eds), *Convergence of Productivity: Cross National Studies in Historical Evidence* (Oxford, 1994), pp. 285–315; E. Abe and R. Fitzgerald, 'Japanese Economic Success: Timing, Culture, and Organisational Capability', in E. Abe and R. Fitzgerald (eds), *The Origins of Japanese Industrial Power: Strategy, Institutions and the Development of Organisational Capability* (London, 1995), pp. 1–31.

26 Chandler, *Scale and Scope*, pp. 9–14.

27 Jones and Rose, *Family Capitalism*; Church, 'Limitations of the Personal Capitalism Paradigm'; Y. Cassis, *Big Business: the European Experience in the Twentieth Century* (Oxford, 1997), pp. 164–8; R. Fitzgerald, *Rowntree and the Marketing Revolution* (Cambridge, England), pp. 185–216.

28 Chandler, *Scale and Scope*, pp. 230–1. See also N. Fligstein, *The Transformation of Corporate Control* (Cambridge, Mass., 1990); E. Sanders, 'Industrial Concentration, Sectional Competition and Antitrust Politics in America, 1880–1980', in K. Oren and S. Skowronek (eds), *Studies in American Political Development*, Vol. 1 (Yale, 1994), pp. 142–213.

29 R. Bendix, *Work, Authority and Industry: Ideologies of Management in the Course of Industrialisation* (New York, 1963); A. A. Berle, and G. C. Means, *The Modern Corporation and Private Property* (New York, 1932).

30 Cassis, *Big Business*, pp. 164–8; Fitzgerald, *Rowntree and the Marketing Revolution*, pp. 185–210; Y. Cassis, 'Divergence and Convergence in British and French Business in the Nineteenth and Twentieth Centuries', and R. Fitzgerald, 'Ownership, Organisation, and Management: British Business and the Branded Consumer Goods Industries', in Y. Cassis, F. Crouzet and T. R. Gourvish, *Business and Management in Britain and France: the Age of the Corporate Economy* (Oxford, 1995), pp. 1–51.

31 Fruin, *Japanese Enterprise System*; Gerlach, *Alliance Capitalism*; G. C. Hamilton and N. W. Biggart, 'Markets, cultures and authority: a comparative analysis of management and organisation in the Far East', *American Journal of Sociology*, vol. 94 (1988), pp. 52–94; M. Aoki and R. Dore (eds), *The Japanese Firm: Sources of Competitive Strength* (Oxford, 1994).

32 J. Hirschmeier and T. Yui, *The Development of Japanese Business, 1600–1973* (London, 1975); K. Nagakawa (ed), *The Strategy and Structure of Big Business* (Tokyo, 1975); K. Kobayashi and H. Morikawa (eds), *Development of Managerial Enterprise* (Tokyo, 1986); H. Morikawa, *Zaibatsu* (Tokyo, 1992); Y. Suzuki, *Japanese Management Structures, 1920–1980* (London, 1991); Fruin, *Japanese Enterprise System*. See also K. Yamamura, 'The Industrialisation of Japan: Entrepreneurship, Ownership and Management', in P. Mathias and M. M. Postan (eds), *The Cambridge Economic History of Europe*, Vol. VII, Part II (Cambridge, England, 1978).

33 See Morikawa, *Zaibatsu*, pp. xxiii–iv; Fruin, *Japanese Enterprise System*, pp. 3–4.

34 Most notably, Chandler, Amatori and Hikino, *Big Business*, and, in particular, H. Morikawa, 'Japan: Increasing Organisational Capabilities of Large Industrial Enterprises, 1880s–1980s', pp. 307–35. See also H. Morikawa, 'The Role of Managerial Enterprises in Post-War Japan's Economic Growth: Focus on the 1950s', in Abe and Fitzgerald (eds), *Origins of Japanese Industrial Power*, pp. 32–43; T. Okazaki, 'The Japanese Firm under the Wartime Planned Economy', in M. Aoki and R. Dore (eds), *The Japanese Firm* (Oxford, 1994), pp. 350–91.

35 Morikawa, *Zaibatsu*, pp. xxiii–iv.

36 See Fruin, *Japanese Enterprise System*.

37 U. Wegenroth, "Germany: Competition Abroad – Co-operation at Home, 1870–1990", in Chandler, Amatori and Hikino (eds), p. 142.

38 Vickers bought a 50 per cent stake.

39 Glasgow Business Records Centre (hereafter GBRC), UGD100/1/1/1, Beardmore, Board Meeting, 15 Jan 1906.

40 GBRC, UGD100/1/1/15, Beardmore, Meeting of Directors, 19 Feb 1929, 3 May 1929. Seealso Tolliday, *Business, Banking and Politics*, pp. 87–8. In 1902, Beardmore also acquired shipbuilders R. Napier & Sons. See Macrosty, *Trust Movement in British Industry*, p. 42.

41 J. R. Hume and M. S. Moss, *Beardmore: the History of a Scottish Giant* (London, 1979), p. 88.

42 'William Beardmore, Jnr, Lord Invernairn', *Dictionary of Scottish Business Biography*, Vol. I (Aberdeen, 1986), pp. 91–3.

43 D. Todd, *The World Shipbuilding Industry* (London, 1985), pp. 36–42, 162, 252–86. See also J R. Parkinson, *The Economics of Shipbuilding in the United Kingdom* (Cambridge, England, 1960); J. R. Parkinson, 'Shipbuilding', in N. Buxton and D. H. Aldcroft (eds), *British Industry between the Wars: Instability and Industrial Development* (London, 1979), pp. 80–4.

44 GBRC, UGD100/1/1/15, Beardmore, Meetings of Directors, 16 Oct 1928.

45 'Sir Thomas Bell', *Dictionary of Scottish Business Biography*, Vol. I (Aberdeen, 1986), pp. 207–211.

46 A. Slaven, 'Management and Shipbuilding, 1890–1938: Structure and Strategy in the Shipbuilding Firm on the Clyde', in A. Slaven and D. H. Aldcroft (eds), *Business, Banking and Urban History* (Edinburgh, 1982), pp. 35–53; E. Lorenz and F. Wilkinson, 'The Shipbuilding Industry, 1880–1965', in B. Elbaum and W. Lazonick, *Decline of the British Economy*, pp. 110–12.

47 GBRC, UGD100/7/1/17, Beardmore, Notes for M. Norman, 16 June 1929.

48 GBRC, UGD100/1/1/15, Beardmore, Meeting of Directors, 4 Sept 1931, 1 June 1931, 27 Nov 1931.

49 GBRC, UGD100/1/1/15, Meetings of Directors, 15 Feb 1928, 7 Feb 1930, 28 Feb 1930, 27 June 1930.

50 GBRC, UGD100/1/1/15, Beardmore, Meetings of Directors, 8 Dec 1930, 27 Nov 1931.

51 Tolliday, *Business, Banking and Politics*, pp. 237–47.

52 Chandler, *Scale and Scope*, pp. 341, 343–4; Tolliday, *Business, Banking and Politics*, pp. 241–7; GBRC, UGD100/1/13/19, Beardmore, Meetings of Directors, 31 Dec 1942; UGD100/1/1/3. Board Minutes, 5 Jan 1950.

53 GBRC, UGD100/1/1/15, Beardmore, Meeting of Directors, 20 Sept 1929, 5 Feb 1930, 28 March 1930, 4 Sept 1931, 16 Dec 1931.

54 'Vickers, Thomas Edward (1833–1915) and Vickers, Albert (1838–1919)', *Dictionary of Business Biography*, Vol. V (London, 1986), pp. 622–8. See also J. Singleton, 'The Tank Producers: British Mechanical Engineering in the Great War', *Journal of Industrial History*, vol. 1 (1998), pp. 88–106; R. P. T. Davenport-Hines, *Dudley Docker: the Life and Times of a Trade Warrior* (Cambridge, England, 1986).

55 See 'Caillard, Sir Vincent Henry Penalvar (1856–1930)', *Dictionary of Business Biography*, Vol. I (London, 1984), pp. 564–8.

56 As is well known, Wolseley was sold to Morris Motors in 1925; the electrical equipment section of Metro-Vick was bought by General Electric in 1928, which merged it with British Thomson-Houston to form Associated Electrical Industries (AEI); the carriage section of Metro-Vick was joined with a similar Cammell Laird operation to form Metro-Cammell Carriage Railway & Wagon Company; the steel-making plants of Vickers and Cammell Laird became the basis of the English Steel Corporation.

57 Chandler, *Scale and Scope*, 341–4; J. D. Scott, *Vickers: a History* (London, 1962), pp. 76–94, 137–68, 158–9. See also C. Trebilcock, *The Vickers Brothers: Armaments and Enterprise, 1854–1914* (London, 1977), pp. ix–xl, 26–51, 142–52.

58 Tolliday, *Business, Banking and Politics*, pp. 191–7.

59 Chandler, *Scale and Scope*, pp. 241–2; J. Dummelow, *1899-1949: Metro-Vickers Electrical Company Ltd* (Manchester, 1949), pp. 2–74.

60 Scott, *Vickers*, pp. 88–94, 152–5, 161–8; Chandler, *Scale and Scope*, pp. 340–5; W. J. Reader, *Bowater: a History* (Cambridge, 1981), pp. 32–59; Tolliday, *Business, Banking and Politics*, pp. 192–7; Trebilcock, *Vickers Brothers*,

pp. xxvi–vii, 146–8. See also S. Pollard and P. L. Robertson, *The British Shipbuilding Industry, 1890–1914* (London, 1979); R. J. Irving, 'New Industries for Old? Some Investment Decisions of Sir W. G. Armstrong, Whitworth & Co. Ltd, 1900–1914', *Business History*, vol. 27 (1975); P. L. Robertson, 'Shipping and shipbuilding: the case of William Denny and Brothers', *Business History*, vol. 16 (1974), pp. 36–47; and R. Craig, 'William Gray and Company: a West Hartlepool shipbuilding enterprise, 1864–1913' in P. L. Cottrell and D. Aldcroft, eds, *Shipping, Trade and Commerce 1450–1914* (Leicester, 1981), pp. 165–191.

61 'Sir Thomas Bell', *Dictionary of Scottish Business Biography*, Vol. I (Aberdeen, 1986), pp. 207–11; A Slaven, 'A shipyard in depression: John Browns of Clydebank', *Business History*, xix (1977), pp. 192–217.

62 'Sir James Lithgow', *Dictionary of Scottish Business Biography*, Vol. I (Aberdeen, 1986), pp. 222–7.

63 Boyce, *Information, Mediation and Institutional Development*, pp. 179, 183–4, 188–94.

64 GBRC, UGD4/12/3, A. Stephen & Co., Minute Book, 30 July 1919, 19 Aug 1920, 20 July 1922, 21 Aug 1922, 20 July 1926, 6 July 1927, 27 June 1929. See also S. L. Jones, 'The Overseas Trading Company in Britain: the Case of the Inchcape Group', in S. Yonekawa and H. Yoshihara (eds), *Business History of General Trading Companies* (Tokyo, 1987), pp. 131–69; S. L. Jones, *Two Centuries of Overseas Trading: the Origins and Growth of the Inchcape Group* (London, 1986); 'Sir Alexander Murray Stephen', *Dictionary of Scottish Business Biography*, Vol. I (Aberdeen, 1986), pp. 238–40.

65 See W. J. Reader, *The Weir Group: A Centenary History* (London, 1971).

66 See E. H. H. Green and M. Moss, *A Business of National Importance: the Royal Mail Shipping Group, 1902–1937* (London, 1982). Royal Mail owned a number of lines, including White Star, and accounted for 15 per cent of Britain's merchant fleet by the early 1930s. Harland and Wolff had a long-standing arrangement to build for White Star and not for its chief rival, Cunard, leading eventually to board links, an exchange of shares, and acquisition. See Boyce, *Information, Mediation and Institutional Development*, pp. 185–7.

67 M. Moss and J. R. Hume, *Shipbuilders to the World: 125 years of Harland and Wolff, Belfast, 1861–1986* (Belfast, 1986), pp. 92, 96–7, 132–3, 135, 173–4, 244–50, 270, 278, 282–3, 285–321; T. R. Gourvish, 'British Business and the Transition to a Corporate Economy: Entrepreneurship and Management Structures', *Business History*, vol. 29 (1987), p. 32.

68 See 'Sir John Craig', *Dictionary of Scottish Business Biography*, Vol. I (Aberdeen, 1986), pp. 101–104.

69 P. L. Payne, *Colvilles and the Scottish Steel Industry* (Oxford, 1979), pp. 188–9, 191–3, 220–2, 238–49, 356. By 1935, Colvilles controlled 80 per cent of Scottish steel output.

70 See A. R. Holmes and E. Green, *Midland. 150 Years of Banking History* (London, 1986), pp. 184–5.

71 'Sir James Lithgow', *Dictionary of Scottish Business Biography*, Vol. I (Aberdeen, 1986), pp. 222–7; Chandler, *Scale and Scope*, pp. 327–8; GBRC, UGD100/1/1/18, 13 April 1939.

72 Boyce, *Information, Mediation and Institutional Development*, pp. 176–8; BPP1918 C.9092 xiii 473.

73 P. L. Payne, 'Industrial Entrepreneurship and Management in Great Britain', in P. Mathias and M. M. Postan (eds), *The Cambridge Economic History of Europe*, Vol. VII, Pt. 1 (Cambridge, England, 1978), pp. 215–9.

74 P. L. Payne, 'Family business in Britain: an Historical and Analytical Survey', in A. Okochi and S. Yasuoka (eds), *Family Business in the Era of Industrial Growth* (Tokyo, 1984), p. 197.

75 See Chandler, *Scale and Scope*; and Lazonick, *Business Organisation*.

76 Morikawa, *Zaibatsu*, pp. 150–2. The new *zaibatsu* were more positive in their policies towards the heavy and chemicals industries.

77 Hannah, 'Visible and Invisible Hands in Great Britain', in Chandler and Daems (eds), *Managerial Hierarchies*, pp. 53, 55–6, 63–4, 87; L. Hannah, 'Strategy and Structure in the Manufacturing Sector', in Hannah (ed.), *Management Strategy and Business Development*, pp. 87, 199. The difficulties of interpreting managerial strength are illustrated by Hannah's strong condemnation of steelmaker Stewart and Lloyds, and by Chandler's more recent praise of that company. See Chandler, *Scale and Scope*, pp. 323–4.

78 Chandler, *Scale and Scope*, pp. 320–5, 327; 'Sir John Craig', *Dictionary of Scottish Business Biography*, Vol. I (Aberdeen, 1986), pp. 101–104; 'Sir Allan Campbell Macdiarmid', *Dictionary of Scottish Business Biography*, Vol. I (Aberdeen, 1986), pp. 121–5; P. W. S. Andrews and E. Brunner, *Capital Development in Steel: a Study of the United Steel Companies* (Oxford, 1951), pp. 119–21, 123–4, 156–8, 162–5, 167–9, 208, 234, 355; R. Peddie, *The United Steel Companies Ltd, 1918–1968* (Manchester, 1969), pp. 13–15, 18–19, 26; F. Scopes, *The Development of the Corby Works* (Portsmouth, 1968), pp. 110–18, 129–31, 237; R. Fitzgerald, *British Labour Management and Industrial Welfare, 1846–1939* (London, 1988), pp. 89–114, 164–72, 184–95; GC. Allen, *British Industries and their Organization* (London, 1959), pp. 155-6, 160-8; J.R. Parkinson, 'Shipbuilding', pp. 79-102.

79 Chandler, *Scale and Scope*, p. 341.

80 Hannah, *Rise of the Corporate Economy*, pp. 8–40. A total of 330, out of 1895 firms affected by mergers between 1887–1900, were to be found in the textile industry: see L. Hannah, 'Mergers in British Manufacturing Industry, 1880–1918', *Oxford Economic Papers*, vol. xxvi (1974), p. 22.

81 Payne, 'Family Business in Britain: an Historical and Analytical Survey", in Okochi and Yasuoka (eds), *Family Business*, p. 181.

82 D. J. Jeremy, 'Survival Strategies in Lancashire textiles: Bleachers' Association Ltd to Whitecroft plc, 1900–1980s', *Textile History*, vol. 24 (1993), pp. 163–209. See also Macrosty, *Trust Movement*, pp. 124–32.

83 Horrockses, Crewdson & Co. was itself an amalgamation of two concerns in 1887. See Macrosty, *Trust Movement*, p. 125.

84 Chandler, *Scale and Scope*, pp. 22–4, 45–6, 288–9, 332–4.

85 S. Chapman, *The Lancashire Cotton Industry: A Study in Economic Development* (Manchester, 1904); S. Chapman and T. Ashton, 'The Sizes of Business Mainly in the Textile Industries', *Journal of the Royal Statistical Society*, vol. lxxvii (1914); Marshall, *Industry and Trade*, pp. 286, 602.

86 G. Jones, *Increasing Return* (Cambridge, 1933); D. Farnie, *The English Cotton Industry and the World Market, 1815–1896* (Oxford, 1979); W. Lazonick, *Competitive Advantage on the Shopfloor* (Cambridge, Mass., 1990); P. Sunley, 'Marshallian Industrial Districts: the Case of the Lancashire Cotton Industry in

the Inter-War Years', *Transactions of the Institute of British Geographers*, vol. 17 (1992), pp. 306–20.

87 See, for example, C. Clark, 'Why Isn't the Whole World Developed? Lessons from the Cotton Mills', *Journal of Economic History*, vol. xlvii (1987), pp. 141–73; M. Mass and W. Lazonick, 'The British Cotton Industry and International Competitive Advantage: the State of the Debates', in M. B. Rose (ed.), *International Competition and Strategic Response in the Textile Industries since 1870* (1990), pp. 9–65; J. Singleton, *World Textile Industry* (London, 1997), pp. 98–101, 127–31. It is worth mentioning that the international trading network of the British textile industry appeared by the inter-war years a poor competitor to larger scale, more organised marketing by other countries. See Department of Overseas Trade, *Report of the British Economic Mission in the Far East* (HMSO, 1931), pp. 240–1.

88 GBRC, UGD143/1/1/1, Linen Thread Company, Copies of Agreements, 17 Dec 1897, 19 May 1898; UGD143/1/3/1, Committee Minutes, 6 July 1898, 23 Sept 1898, 14 Oct 1898, 22 June 1898, 30 Dec 1898, 26 Jan 1899, 22 Feb 1899, 7 March 1899, 27 April 1899, 6 July 1899, 7 July 1899; UGD143/1/3/2, Committee Minutes, 9 Aug 1899, 13 Sept 1899; UGD143/5/4, Executive Committee, 1901–46, 24 Dec 1901, 13 June 1902, 9 Dec 1902. See also Linen Thread Company, *The Faithful Fibre* (privately published, 1951). Further reorganisation occurred in 1953, when the company and its subsidiaries were placed in groups based on products. See UGD143/1/3/47, Board Minutes, 16 April 1953, 16 July 1953.

89 J. Clapham, *An Economic History of Modern Britain*, Vol. III (Cambridge, England, 1951), pp. 229, 231, 289; 'Sir Alfred Herbert Dixon, Bart (1857–1920)', *Dictionary of Business Biography*, Vol. II (London, 1984), pp. 107–10; 'Broadhurst, Sir Edward Tootal', *Dictionary of Business Biography*, Vol. V (London, 1984); 'Douglas, George', *Dictionary of Business Biography*, Vol. II (London, 1984); 'Lee, Henry (1817–1904), and Lee, Sir Joseph Cocksey (1832–1894)', *Dictionary of Business Biography*, Vol. III (London, 1985), pp. 703–14; 'Lee, Lennox Bertram (1864–1949)', *Dictionary of Business Biography*, Vol. III (London, 1985), pp. 715–25; P. L. Cook and R. Cohen, *Effects of Mergers: Six Studies* (London, 1958), pp. 151–68.

90 Payne, 'Emergence of the Large-Scale Company in Great Britain'; Payne, 'Family Business in Britain', in Okochi and Yasuoka (eds), *Family Business*, p. 181; D. W. Kim, 'From a Family Partnership to a Corporate Company: J. & P. Coats, Thread Manufacturers', *Textile History*, vol. 25 (1994), pp. 185–226; A. K. Cairncross and J. B. K. Hunter, 'The early growth of Messrs J. & P. Coats, 1830–1883', *Business History*, vol. 29 (1987).

91 Chandler, *Scale and Scope*, p. 289.

92 'Archibald Coats', *Dictionary of Scottish Business Biography*, Vol. I (Aberdeen, 1986), pp. 329–35; 'Sir James Henderson', *Dictionary of Scottish Business Biography*, Vol. I (Aberdeen, 1986), pp. 363–6; 'Otto Ernst Philippi', *Dictionary of Scottish Business Biography*, Vol. I (Aberdeen, 1986), pp. 389–92; Macrosty, *Trust Movement*, pp. 144–54.

93 Macrosty, pp. 121–36, 137–49, 151.

94 'Archibald Coats', *Dictionary of Scottish Business Biography*, Vol. I (Aberdeen, 1986), pp. 329–35; 'Sir James Henderson', *Dictionary of Scottish Business Biography*, Vol. I (Aberdeen, 1986), pp. 363–6; 'Otto Ernst Philippi',

Dictionary of Scottish Business Biography, Vol. I (Aberdeen, 1986), pp. 389–92; Macrosty, *Trust Movement*, pp. 144–54.

95 GBRC, UGD143/1/3/1, Linen Thread Company, Committee Minutes, 26 June 1898, 7 March 1899; Macrosty, *Trust Movement*, pp. 136–7.

96 'Otto Ernst Philippi', *Dictionary of Scottish Business Biography*, Vol. I (Aberdeen, 1986), p. 391.

97 GBRC, UGD199/1/1/5, J. & P. Coats, Directors' Minute Book, 1928–38, 27 July 1928, 9 Oct 1930, 12 Nov 1930, 13 Nov 1930, 11 June 1931, 25 May 1933, 19 July 1934, 11 June 1936, 16 July 1937, 7 Dec 1936; UGD199/1/1/14, General Purposes Committee, 1930–1936, 23 Oct 1930, 24 Oct 1930, 21 Nov 1930, 27 Nov 1930; UGD199/1/1/59, Organisation Committee, 14 Oct 1931, 11 Nov 1931, 9 Dec 1931, 29 Dec 1931, 13 Jan 1932, 4 March 1932, 17 March 1932, 7 Dec 1932, 14 March 1933, 18 April 1933, 13 June 1933, 19 Dec 1933; UGD199/1/1/74, Executive Committee: Division 1, 1930–1945, 9 Dec 1930;

98 D. A. Farnie and S. Yonekawa, 'The Emergence of the Large Firm in the Cotton Spinning Industries of the World, 1883–1938', *Textile History*, vol. 19 (1988), pp. 171–210. Despite the unwillingness of Lancashire textile firms to merge or co-operate over sales or purchasing, they demonstrated a high degree of joint action in collective bargaining arrangements. See A. J. McIvor, *Organised Capital: Employers' Associations and Industrial Relations in Northern England, 1880–1939* (Cambridge, England, 1996).

99 M. A. Utton, 'Some Features of the Early Merger Movements in British Manufacturing Industry', *Business History*, vol. 14 (1972), pp. 51–60.

100 W. Lazonick, 'The Cotton Industry', in Elbaum and Lazonick (eds), *Decline of the British Economy*, pp. 18–50; W. Lazonick, 'Industrial Organisation and Technological Change: the Decline of the British Cotton Industry', *Business History Review*, vol. 107 (1983), pp. 230–6; Allen, *British Industries*, pp. 211-52; M. W. Kirby, 'The Lancashire Cotton Industry in the Inter-War Years: a Study in Organisational Change', *Business History*, vol. 26 (1974), pp. 145–59; J.H. Porter, 'Cotton and Wool Textiles', in Buxton and Aldcroft (eds), *British Industry*, pp. 25-47; J. H. Bamberg, 'The Rationalisation of the British Cotton Industry in the Interwar Years', *Textile History*, vol. 19 (1988), pp. 83–102.

101 Morikawa, *Zaibatsu*, pp. 1–2, 43, 114, 215; Suzuki, *Japanese Management Structures*, pp. 50, 54.

102 'Nippon Yusen Kabushiki Kaisha', *International Directory of Company Histories*, vol. 4 (London, 1991), pp. 481–3. See also W. D. Wray, *Mitsubishi and NYK* (Harvard, 1984). During the general sale of state assets, Mitsubishi bought the Nagasaki shipyard in 1887.

103 'Nippon Yusen Kabushiki Kaisha', *International Directory of Company Histories*, vol. 4 (London, 1991), pp. 481–3. See also W. D. Wray, *Mitsubishi and NYK* (Harvard, 1984).

104 The forerunner of Kawasaki Steel Corporation. See Morikawa, *Zaibatsu*, p. 130; E. Abe, "Anatomy of a Japanese Steel Firm: NKK – Its Strategy and Performance against the Tide, 1951–1990", in T. Yuzawa (ed.), *Japanese Business Success: the Evolution of a Strategy* (London, 1994), pp. 65–80.

105 Morikawa, *Zaibatsu*, pp. 1–24, 57–92, 146–7; 'Mitsubishi Heavy Industries', *International Directory of Company Histories*, Vol. 4 (London, 1991), pp. 577–9; 'Kawasaki Heavy Industries Ltd', *International Directory of Company Histories*, Vol. 4 (London, 1991), pp. 538–40.

106 K. Yamazaki, 'Mitsui Bussan during the 1920s', in A. Teichova, M. Levy-Leboyer and H. Nussbaum (eds), *Historical Studies in International Corporate Business* (Cambridge, England, 1989).

107 Morikawa, *Zaibatsu*, pp. 1–24, 57–92, 106–14, 126, 128, 130, 145–6, 183, 192; M. Miyamoto, 'The Position and Role of the Family Business in the Development of the Japanese Company System', in Okochi and Yasuoka (eds), *Family business*, pp. 39–94; M. Shimotani, "History and Structure of Business Groups", in Shiba and Shimotani (eds), *Beyond the Firm*, p. 17.

108 Morikawa, *Zaibatsu*, pp. 106–14, 183, 192; M. Miyamoto, 'The Position and Role of the Family Business in the Development of the Japanese Company System', in Okochi and Yasuoka (eds), *Family business*, pp. 39–94; M. Shimotani, "History and Structure of Business Groups", in Shiba and Shimotani (eds), *Beyond the Firm*, p. 17.

109 See 'Kawasaki Kisen Kaisha, Ltd', *International Directory of Company Histories*, Vol. 4 (London, 1991), pp. 457–60.

110 Y. Fukasaku, *Technology and Industrial Development in Pre-War Japan: Mitsubishi Nagasaki Shipyard, 1884–1934* (London, 1992), pp. 12–42; Morikawa, *Zaibatsu*, pp. 121–130, 140–158; Todd, *World Shipbuilding Industry*, pp. 286–96. See also 'Sumitomo Heavy Industries Ltd', *International Directory of Company Histories*, Vol. 4 (London, 1991), pp. 634–5; 'Mitsui O. S. K. Lines Ltd', *International Directory of Company Histories*, Vol. 4 (London, 1991), pp. 473–6.

111 Morikawa, *Zaibatsu*, pp. 1–24, 57–92, 146–7; 'Mitsubishi Heavy Industries', *International Directory of Company Histories*, Vol. 4 (London, 1991), pp. 577–9; 'Kawasaki Heavy Industries Ltd', *International Directory of Company Histories*, Vol. 4 (London, 1991), pp. 538–40. See also T. Chida and P. N. Davies, *The Japanese Shipping and Shipbuilding Industries* (London, 1990).

112 Suzuki, *Japanese Management Structures*, pp. 33–6. See also T. Yui, 'Development, organisation, and business strategy of industrial enterprises in Japan, 1915–1935', *Japanese Yearbook on Business History*, vol. 5 (1988).

113 Suzuki, *Japanese Management Structures*, pp. 33–4.

114 Morikawa, *Zaibatsu*, pp. 182–248; Shimotani, 'History and Structure of Business Groups in Japan'; K. Suzuki, 'From *Zaibatsu* to Corporate Complexes'; and T. Shiba, 'A Path to the Corporate Group in Japan: Mitsubishi Heavy Industries and its Group Formation', in Shiba and Shimotani (eds), *Beyond the Firm*, pp. 5–28, 59–87, 167–84; T. Okazaki, 'The Japanese Firm under the Wartime Planned Economy', in Aoki and Dore (eds), *The Japanese Firm*, pp. 350–78.

115 Yui, "Development, Organisation, and Business Strategy".

116 D. Farnie and S. Yonekawa, 'The Emergence of the Largest Firms in the Cotton Spinning Industries of the World, 1883–1938', *Textile History*, vol. 19 (1988).

117 Yui, 'Development, Organisation, and Business Strategy'; T. Yui, 'The Enterprise System in Japan: Preliminary Considerations on Internal and External Relations', *Japanese Yearbook on Business History*, vol. 8 (1991); Shimotani, 'History and Structure of Business Groups', pp. 2, 5–7, 11–14.

118 Suzuki, *Japanese Management Structures*, pp. 26–8, 33, 35–6.

119 Chandler, *Scale and Scope*, pp. 231–2, 488–96, 506–7, 550–61, 587–92. See also Wengenroth, 'Germany: Competition Abroad – Co-operation at Home'; G. P. Dyas and H. T. Thannheiser, *The Emerging European Enterprise: Strategy and Structure in French and German Industry* (London, 1976); V. Berghahn

(ed.), *German Big Business and Europe, 1914–1993* (1994); W. Feldenkirchen, 'Business Groups in the German Electrical Industry', in Shiba and Shimotani (eds), *Beyond the Firm*, pp. 135–66; S. Hilger, 'Welfare Policy in German Big Business after the First World War: Vereinigte Stahlwerke AG, 1926–33', *Business History*, vol. 40 (1998), pp. 50–76; J. Kocka, 'The Rise of the Modern Industrial Enterprise in Germany', in Chandler and Daems (eds), *Managerial Hierarchies*, pp. 77–116.

120 Wegenroth, 'Germany: Competition Abroad – Cupertino at Home', pp. 142, 149–51.

121 See Fruin, *Japanese Enterprise System*.

122 H. Daems, *The Holding Company and Corporate Control* (Leiden, 1978), pp. 1-5, 34, 137; S. Kurgan-Van Hentenryk, 'Structure and Strategy of Belgium Business Groups (1920-1990)', in Shiba and Shimotani (eds), *Beyond the Firm*, pp.88-108.

123 R. Coase, 'The Nature of the Firm', *Economica*, vol. 4 (1937), pp. 386–405; O. E. Williamson, *Markets and Hierarchies* (New York, 1975); O. E. Williamson, *The Economic Institutions of Capitalism* (New York, 1985).

124 O. Westall and A. C. Goodal, *Business History and Business Culture* (Manchester, 1996).

125 P. Scranton, 'Diversity in Diversity: Production and American Industrialisation, 1880–1930', *Business History Review*, vol. 65 (1991), pp. 27–90; P. Scranton, *Endless Novelty: Specialty Production and American Industrialisation, 1865–1925* (Princeton, 1997); P. Scranton, '"Have a Heart for the Manufacturers!": Production, Deistribution, and the Decline of American Textile Manufacturing', in Sabel and Zeitlin, *World of Possibilities*, pp. 310–43.

126 See C. A. Bartlett and S. Ghoshal, 'Beyond the M-Form: Towards a Managerial Theory of the Firm', *Strategic Management Journal*, vol. 4 (1993), pp. 23–46; C. A. Bartlett, 'Building and Managing the Transnational: the New Organisational Challenge', in M. E. Porter (ed.), Competition in Global Industries (Harvard, 1986), pp. 367–404. See also D. J. Teece, 'The Dynamics of Industrial Capitalism: Perspectives on Alfred Chandler's *Scale and Scope*', *Journal of Economic Literature*, vol. 31 (1993), pp. 199–225.

127 See J. Pfeffer and G. Salancik, *The External Control of Organizations: A Resource Dependence Perspective* (New York, 1978); A. Goto, 'Business Groups in a Market Economy', *European Economic Review*, vol. 19 (1982), pp. 53–70.

128 Boyce, *Information, Mediation and Institutional Development*, 198–200, 206–20, 223–62, 265–311.

129 Fitzgerald, *Rowntree and the Marketing Revolution*, pp. 204–5; Fitzgerald, 'Markets, Management and Merger: John Mackintosh & Sons, 1890–1969', forthcoming.

130 I am thankful to John Wilson for offering these points. See J. Wilson, 'The Holding Company Movement in British Gas Supply and the United Kingdom Gas Corporation: Motivation, Organisation and Impact' (unpublished paper).

131 L. Hannah, *Electricity before Nationalization: A Study of the Development of the Supply Industry to 1948* (London, 1979), pp. 227–234.

132 Hannah, 'Visible and Invisible Hands in Great Britain', in Chandler and Daems (eds), *Managerial Hierarchies*, pp. 53, 55–6, 63–4, 87; L. Hannah, 'Strategy and Structure in the Manufacturing Sector', in Hannah (ed.), *Management Strategy and Business Development*, pp. 87, 199.

133 See N. Leff, 'Capital Markets in the Less Developed Countries: the Group Principle', in R. McKinnon (ed.), *Money and Finance in Economic Growth and Development* (New York, 1976), pp. 97–122; N. Leff, 'Industrial Organisation and Entrepreneurship in the Developing Countries: the Economic Groups', *Economic Development and Cultural Change*, vol. 26 (1978), pp. 661–75.

2 Debates and Speculations

Reflections on Robert Fitzgerald on Holding Companies

John Quail

Historians live by the new and revisionism is the spring rain of academe from which new thoughts grow. For all that, it was brave of Robert Fitzgerald to consider the possible fertility of pre-World War Two UK holding companies in the *Journal of Industrial History*, volume 3 (2000) number 2. I agree with his argument that the flexible potential of the holding company form has been underestimated. I agree that 'holding company' can be too readily used as a form of 'two legs bad' as opposed to managerial hierarchy's 'four legs good'. I cannot agree, though, that this potential flexibility was demonstrated by UK firms except in exceptional cases. On the contrary the significant thing about the use UK business made of holding companies is precisely the lack of innovation. Lack of innovation was, indeed, not restricted to holding companies but also amply demonstrated by the allegedly more 'progressive' large UK unitary joint stock companies.[1] I would suggest that the important question remains, therefore, why – not whether – there was this failure to innovate.

Fitzgerald is right to remind us about the positive role holding companies played in the development of large UK business. They were indeed a cheap and cheerful way of combining companies – particularly when the proportion of ordinary shares to preferred shares and loan stocks was low, as was often the case.[2] They were not in themselves a restrictive form of organisation and UK company law seems to have been highly permissive, if not indifferent as far as forms of corporate governance were concerned. Fitzgerald could, in fact, have gone far further in his claims for the adaptability of the holding company form, a spectacular if isolated example being Unilever. The comparison Fitzgerald makes between UK and Japanese company practice is interesting, but is the point at which we start to diverge. The difficulty is that this comparison invites us to assume a virtue by association for UK companies (or at least a plea in mitigation) which will lead us to look elsewhere for the causes of the UK's lack of corporate competitiveness. After all, if Japanese companies adopted a similar form to UK companies,

DOI: 10.4324/9781003313397-3

then, given Japan's subsequent global corporate success, UK companies had chosen their company structure well. This being the case, it is suggested, any problems there have been with corporate competitiveness are due to external factors.

In fact, Japanese holding companies differed from their UK counterparts in origin, intention and corporate 'glue'. They were the means of formalising diverse family businesses in the case of the Zaibatsu or for large companies more generally a way of diversifying into new areas or integrating businesses backwards or forwards. The intention appears to have been to grow new or acquired companies to the point at which they became viable, at which point parent control appears to have been relaxed. The affiliations between companies appear to have been as much clan loyalty as ownership, particularly in the Zaibatsu.[3] There is no particularly close comparison with UK holding companies where many mergers were horizontal, defensive and anti-competitive and integrated to the extent required only to survive.

The key problem, which his closing discussion does hint at, is that UK companies, with a few exceptions, did not adapt the adaptable and by implication could not use the opportunities that the holding company form presented in the way that Japanese companies could. We must ask, then, whether the problem is the holding company form or the use of that form by UK companies. This question puts UK companies back in the dock as far as corporate competitiveness and (ultimately) UK relative economic decline is concerned. It also raises questions about the institutional/cultural causes of rigidity in UK company structure which take us well beyond issues of random choice.

The holding company in the UK, it has been argued by Payne, Chandler and others,[4] generally served the particular organisational purposes of the controllers of the individual firms which were brought together. Fitzgerald argues that the companies he surveys changed and adapted. I do not think that Payne or Chandler would disagree. It can be asked, however, whether the response to the need for change was reluctant and minimal or enthusiastic and innovatory. The choice between the two approaches is not a simple one. In a mature economy and in mature industries it was inevitable that choices would be constrained by past trading experience and the perceived future prospects for the new larger businesses. The stated aims of pre-World War One amalgamations were generally to control 'cut-throat' competition and were formed for defensive/monopolistic purposes, rather than developmental strategic ends. The organisational capacity of the constituent companies as measured by pre-existing management practice was generally limited and might be expected to constrain post-amalgamation innovations. Even if these circumstances made strategic organisational change and managerial innovation difficult, however, it did not make it impossible. Relevant theoretical writings and managerial practice was available if required.[5] Nevertheless, as far as the great majority of mergers before and after the First World War are concerned I would argue that the changes that were instituted were and remained the bare minimum needed for commercial survival of the new company.[6]

Having said that, however, just how important is that observation? Fitzgerald clearly wishes to argue the value of the holding company as a means of innovation. Even if that proves only barely true, the real test is whether the new amalgamations worked as businesses. It must be admitted that many of the manufacturing amalgamations of the late nineteenth century chronicled by Macrosty appear largely to have met their modest business objectives and survived largely unchanged for many decades.[7] This must count as some form of success. Clearly below some threshold of size, complexity or rate of change, the 'failure' to choose integrated managerial hierarchies is largely irrelevant. Below this threshold relatively loosely amalgamated businesses could survive and even prosper with moderately efficient personal leadership and a certain level of centralisation of purchasing, marketing and management information. The difficulties came when the task of organising a business did cross the threshold of size, complexity or rate of change. This is a crucial test of Fitzgerald's position and an illustrative case is that of Vickers. For this firm the holding company in its federalist form was almost ruinous, and instead of leading to an evolution of organisational structure and method to allow diversification into new expanding sectors brought about instead divestment and a humiliating retreat back to an original core business which was in steep decline.

The most illuminating example is the fate of the Wolseley car firm which Vickers acquired in 1901. The company steadily expanded up to the First World War and was the largest indigenous UK producer with a level of output roughly half the level of Ford's UK plant. There were very clear first-mover advantages: a large integrated plant, substantial investment and a product in tune with the elite market of the time. Yet after World War One matters seem to have collapsed. On the face of it Vickers' World War One experience of armaments mass production, combined with an economic clout greatly enhanced by wartime profits, should have placed Wolseley in the first rank. It did not do so despite the fact that its closest indigenous competitors, Austin and Morris, were severely handicapped. Austin was deeply undercapitalised and nearly went bankrupt. Morris faced considerable problems of post-war readjustment. Yet both firms with minimal outside aid were able to restructure, introduce new mass-produced products and move towards oligopoly as the 1920s progressed. When Morris bought Wolseley in a liquidator's sale in 1927, his sales had expanded from 3000 in 1921 to 55,000. Wolseley's sales were 'little more than a few thousand a year'.[8]

Vickers' involvement in a new technology like motor manufacture in the changing market and economic conditions after World War One was a key test of their ability to expand their technical and managerial capacity. It was now not sufficient to leave local management to get on with it for good or ill which had been the story of the various undigested companies in the Vickers portfolio prior to WW1.[9] It is also clear from other sources that Vickers' managerial and cost control was not well developed.[10] What was now required was a far more active management of their investment from marketing through costing to manufacture. The task was not impossible, but it would have involved a transformation of Vickers' managerial structure and style perhaps comparable to that at General Motors at about the same time. It is clear that Vickers did not attempt the task. The acquisitions by Vickers demonstrated ambition and the will to diversify, but also demonstrates a helplessness in the face of complexity which, given the huge advantages the firm enjoyed, may be taken as emblematic.

It is emblematic because it is not untypical of a certain general refusal among large UK companies to use the advantages they had. This is the chief value of Chandler's litany in *Scale and Scope*: whatever difficulties scholars may have with the concept of 'personal capitalism' or whatever plea in mitigation may be put in by way of reference to external circumstances, the actual performance record of UK companies taken in the round was poor. One important reason why performance was poor was firm structure. It is significant that Hannah, noted as a historian with a very positive view of UK corporate development in the inter-war years, accepted in his review of *Scale and Scope* that firstly there had been widespread entrepreneurial failure, and secondly that this was due to a failure to 'develop managerial hierarchies as deep, or... as well trained and professional as those in America (or in Germany). I find this convincing... one cannot but come to this conclusion as one examines one weak firm after another...'.[11]

The failure of Vickers is thrown into sharp relief when we consider the developmental adaptability of the holding company form as demonstrated by Unilever. Taking over a succession of firms, first Lever Brothers then Unilever (founded September 1929) were not over-concerned to buy out minority or preference shareholders even after a bruising battle with preference shareholders at Gossages in 1931 – 32 demonstrated the risks of this approach.[12] The ordinary shareholdings Unilever/Lever Brothers controlled were sufficient for them to appoint the boards of directors of acquired firms and guaranteed control. The continuing representation on 'their' firms' boards of old family names did not prevent a process of product grouping and divisionalisation in all but name and centralised financial and budgetary control. The process was *conscious*: the product grouping took place very early in the Lever Brothers/Margarine Union merger and the strategy of rationalisation within the UK soap firms, the most anarchic section of the merger, was established by 1931.[13] Effectively, the subsidiary companies withered into husks. What was formally a very large holding company was able to evolve into what was formally a divisionalised structure after World War Two with little apparent difficulty, largely because the new form had matured within the confines of the old. This incidentally reveals the weakness of Chandler's analysis of Unilever, which he characterises as a simple federation of firms only marginally changed from W. H. Lever's pre- and post-World War One acquisition spree remaining 'relatively unchanged after 1932'. This federation, however, had become a fully fledged multi-divisional company by 1946.[14] While this is a plausible reading of Wilson's company history, it makes little sense given Chandler's own emphasis on the difficulty of moving from personal to corporate management in the UK.

The example of Unilever demonstrates what Vickers' diversification might have become but failed to achieve. It shows that personal management and the merger as loosely knit agglomeration were not inevitable in the UK. Nevertheless, it appears to have been the general rule. Smaller-scale amalgamations could survive at a modest level of integration. For companies contemplating amalgamation beyond some level of complexity and size, the problems clearly became acute. As the earlier quotation from Hannah hinted, this was primarily a problem of making the organisational changes necessary to cope with this new complexity and size. The evidence appears to be that UK companies found it extraordinarily difficult to make them. The question must be why?

The question understood broadly is not a new one and a number of answers have been suggested. Some are as much ways of describing the problem as they are explanations: for example, the influence of 'the practical man'[15] or 'personal capitalism'[16] or the 'managerial limits to growth'.[17] The curiously frozen response by companies to some forms of change and not others suggests that cultural or institutional explanations may be more promising. Why is it, for example, that major amalgamations could readily take place which were not without risk to the participants' capital and free-dom of action, yet forms of organisation which increased reliance on pro-fessional managers (thereby increasing the depth of management hierarchy) were utterly unacceptable?[18] We need not accept the specific arguments of Wiener[19] or Elbaum and Lazonick[20] to suggest that cultural and institutional rigidities can have powerful and lasting effects, particularly where they pre-serve and are in turn reinforced by specific relations of power. As I have argued elsewhere,[21] the rights of property were the key ideological under-pinning of joint stock firm structure with a firm line drawn between directors (seen as a committee of owners) and managers (seen as employees requir-ing supervision). The reserved powers of the board to direct and co-ordinate the firm combined with part-time attendance led to the under-development of top management and management technique and, in consequence, limited managerial capacity. (Owner-managed or family dominated firms were paradoxically better able to demonstrate innovation in management technique.[22]) Faced with circumstances where entrepreneurial ambition potentially or actually outran management capacity, organisational change presented itself institutionally as a loss of power by those in charge, culturally, as the overthrow of the proper order of things. The cultural and institutional inertia that had to be overcome if qualitative managerial change was to take place was therefore very great. This was as much the case for unified joint stock companies like railways as it was for loose holding company structures like Vickers. Nevertheless, while the holding company was and remains a flexible and adaptable company form, historically the capacity of the holding company in many UK corporate hands to maximise dysfunction and lack of adaptability means that, despite Fitzgerald's advocacy, the historian's correct first reaction to them will be suspicion.

Notes

1 J. M. Quail, 'Proprietors and Managers: Structure and Technique in Large British Enterprise 1890 to 1939' (unpublished PhD thesis, University of Leeds, 1996); J. M. Quail, 'The Pro-prietorial Theory of the Firm and its Consequences', *Journal of Industrial History*, 3,2 (2000)

2 P. L. Cottrell, *Industrial Finance 1830–1914* (London: Methuen, 1980) p. 62 ff.

3 Y. Suzuki, *Japanese Management Structures 1920–80* (London: Macmillan, 1991) Chapters 2 & 3.

4 See sources cited by J. Wilson, *British Business History 1720–1994* (Manchester University Press, 1995) pp. 154–5; A. D. Chandler, *Scale and Scope* (Cambridge, Mass.: Belknap, 1990) p. 286 ff.

5 See the written sources set out in L. Urwick and E. F. L. Brech, *The Making of Scientific Management Vol. II, Management in British Industry* (London, 1946); some examples of interesting management accounting practice have been brought to light by Boyns and Edwards and their associates with main points summarised in T. Boyns and J. R. Edwards, 'British Cost and Management Accounting Theory and Practice *c*.1850 – *c*.1950, Resolved and Unresolved Issues', *Business and Economic History*, 26,2, Winter 1997.

6 As fn 1.

7 Compare the common firms described in H. W. Macrosty, *The Trust Movement in British Industry* (London: Longmans, 1907) and G. Turner, *Business in Britain* (London: Eyre and Spottiswoode, 1969). See also A. D. Chandler, *Scale and Scope*, p. 291 where a similar point is made.

8 G. Maxcy, 'The Motor Industry' in P. L. Cook and R. Cohen (eds), *Effects of Mergers* (London: George Allen, 1958) p. 367.

9 Macrosty, *Trust Movement*, has the detailed sequence of acquisitions to the early Twentieth Century. See also C. Trebilcock, *Vickers Brothers – Armaments and Enterprise 1854–1914* (London: Europa, 1977); J. R. Hume & M. S. Moss,

Beardmore – The History of a Scottish Industrial Giant (London: Heinemann, 1979); L. Hannah, 'Strategy and Structure in the Manufacturing Sector' in L. Hannah (ed.), *Management Strategy and Business Development* (London: Methuen, 1976).

10 See the War Office survey *Organisation and Accounts of the Ordnance Factories* (1902) at PRO WO 33/240 particularly Appendix 5. See also comments in J. M. Quail, thesis, pp. 59–61.

11 L. Hannah, review of *Scale and Scope, Business History*, 33,2 (April 1991), p. 301.

12 J. M. Quail, thesis, pp. 275–6.

13 J. M. Quail, thesis, p. 270.

14 A. D. Chandler, *Scale and Scope*, p. 378 ff.

15 Robert R. Locke, *The End of Practical Man* (London, 1984).

16 A. D. Chandler, *Scale and Scope*.

17 L. Hannah, *Rise of the Corporate Economy* (London: Methuen, 1983).

18 Examples are the Calico Printers Association reorganisation (J. M. Quail, thesis, pp. 64–7) and the refusal of the North Eastern Railway Board of a managing directorship to George Gibb in 1905 (J. M. Quail, thesis, p. 49).

19 M. J. Wiener, *English Culture and the Decline of the Industrial Spirit* (Cambridge University Press, 1981).

20 B. Elbaum and W. Lazonick (eds), *The Decline of the British Economy* (Oxford: Clarendon Press, 1986), editors introduction.

21 As fn 1

22 J. M. Quail, 'More Peculiarities of the British: Budgetary Control in US and UK Business to 1939', *Business and Economic History*, 26,2 (Winter 1997).

3 Corporate Structures and Holding Companies in Britain

Evidence, Comparison and Appraisal

Robert Fitzgerald

1. British Business and Company Structures

In a recent article on pre-war British business organization,[1] I had two broad objectives. One was to investigate suggestions that holding companies before the Second World War, despite containing parlous examples, did not deserve to be so strongly condemned for their organizational choices. These enterprises being prevalent amongst large-scale business, they were undeniably important to the British economy, and their acknowledged commercial difficulties and choice of organizational form during this period have been seen as evidence of general managerial malaise. If the record warranted some degree of revision, and if their decisions could be rationalised, my second motive was to ask how these accorded with or drew support from current debates on the principles of large-scale business organization. In replying to John Quail's comments, I have the opportunity to clarify and expand on my review of these companies, although I remain as inconclusive or as sceptical about the debate as before. My reservations are partly founded on the nature of the evidence available, partly on the fact I survey only two sectors in detail, and partly because, for particular reasons, I limit myself to the pre-war decades. Few would question the critical role of management, although differences in structure may not receive so much support, but it is possible that both have received too much singular emphasis. In appraising the performance of varying forms, especially within a comparative dimension, consideration has to be given to many other points that have also traditionally been the concern of historians. The internal aspects of a company and the minutiae of organization have to be understood in combination with other, external factors, both in shaping the possibilities for and the consequences of managerial decisions. The same 'rules' apply, without prejudice, to the holding company.

Moreover, the topic of business organization has over the last decade produced a number of important studies that have greatly deepened and

DOI: 10.4324/9781003313397-4

broadened our understanding. Differing perspectives enable us to re-consider the history of management structure. There existed Chandler's two major works on the rise of the U.S. corporation,[2] and an array of Harvard-sponsored studies, extending his thesis to the post-war period, or in addition reviewing the development of multidivisional enterprise in Britain, Germany, France and Italy.[3] The publication of *Scale and Scope* in 1990 was pathbreaking for its international comparison of the U.S., Britain and Germany, and there are few more significant books for management theorists, and probably none for business historians.[4] The book proved seminal because, firstly, it added new information and synthesis, and aroused debate about the nature of corporate management within its three case-studies. Secondly, by engaging in the act of comparison, it reached controversial conclusions about the links between managerial types and a nation's industrial and economic success. It, therefore, raised questions about method, and the validity of applying a managerial model in many differing circumstances, hinting at a universalist versus a contextualised approach. Thirdly, its publication coincided with a growing interest in business organization trends and perspectives less attuned to Chandler's emphasis on transaction costs, synergies in scale and scope, internal management resources, and the multidivisional enterprise. Books and articles noted the examples of de-merger and corporate de-layering, and considered the ramifications of business networks, principal-agent relationships,[5] cultural and institutional 'embeddedness',[6] and non-economic explanations of the multidivisional.[7] One source of this revisionism was expanding knowledge of Japan and Asia, to which business history through Fruin made a notable contribution,[8] followed by Cassis who similarly augmented our knowledge by his study of Europe.[9]

2. Britain and Evidence

On the first issue of debates about evidence and interpretation, British business historians have fairly robustly expressed their doubts about Chandler's concept of 'personal capitalism' as an explanation for industrial failure, stoutly defending the family firm in particular. As well as questioning interpretations of corporate governance in Britain, there is a benefit to re-appraising the evidence. Chandler, for example, begins his analysis with lengthy investigations of 'prototype' companies. On the basis of what we know, his critical analysis of the federated Imperial Tobacco seems fair. But, as I have argued elsewhere,[10] his account of Cadbury appears a misunderstanding, because there is a wealth of archival and other data offering a contrary and more positive viewpoint.

Commentators have also focused attention on business organization within the older industrial sectors, notably shipbuilding and armaments, and textiles. More recent work, including Chandler's, has acknowledged relative success stories and the efforts made by some of these federated firms and holding companies to rationalise and organise. But the overall judgement remains negative. Arguably, the available evidence for several cited cases is not extensive, especially at the level of the subsidiary, or it is open to interpretation; additional information, particularly for the inter-war period, does show a growing attention to matters of organization; there is a pattern and rationale to the development of many holding companies, suited to some degree to their product markets and economic circumstances; the firms demonstrate a variety of choices in management, with mixed results; and many if not all cases reveal a low causal relation with corporate success or failure. Where scale economies were not available, or ignored, scope advantages were available through vertical linkages. A system of subsidiaries offered companies the benefits of rapid growth, diversification, or risk-aversion, and national and local business networks, acting as sources of commercial information and trust relationships, encouraged and supported holding company arrangements. Market knowledge and deal-making required a different type of entrepreneurship to the skills of organization-building. Alongside responses to the 'external' dimension, 'internal' aspects were not ignored: professional managers were appointed, and there are examples of evolving central control and strong management at the subsidiary level. The concentration of support services such as purchasing or accounting within the headquarters function suggests economies and enhanced effectiveness. Overall, holding companies could not or did not systemise 'operational relations' between its units in the manner available to multidivisional forms with strategies of more related diversification. But rapid growth, the spreading of risk, vertical linkages, unrelated diversification, deal-making networks, marketing channels, and information flows were advantages still to be found in various 'corporate relations', with synergies being revealed through the centralization of finance, purchasing, and support services. Finally, outside the 'traditional' or industrial goods sectors, the strategies and operations of holding companies in consumer goods, public utilities, trade or finance expose differing organizational needs and outcomes. Consequently, my comments and those of others before me are not necessarily inimical to the Chandlerian model. They merely extend his own arguments about the managerial relationship between product markets and the 'new' growth industries of the twentieth century. Other sectors may require different 'organizational logics'. Chandler also overlooks the influence of timing and national context, and, while this has emerged as a major criticism, they too could be used to enlarge the horizons of his framework.

John Quail calls my article 'brave', recalling the word used by Sir Humphrey Appleby whenever he dissuaded the politician Jim Hacker from a course of action. Yet I was, as he implies, employing the modestly-stated arguments of others that, however great the worldwide contribution of the multidivisional, generalizations of its aptness have been exaggerated. From Britain to Europe to Asia – and even the U.S. – holding companies have been an important presence, and their existence cannot be entirely accidental or unnatural. I understand that any advantages are contingent or contextual. Indeed, that is a major point of my original article, and, with the same caveat applying to the multidivisional, it is a factor not adequately considered by *Scale and Scope*. In which case, criticisms have to be based on the suggestion that the holding company was particularly deleterious in British conditions, assuming these to have been the same over the last one hundred years or so. I think that this is the gist of John Quail's argument, when he notes 'historically the capacity of the holding company in many UK corporate hands to maximise dysfunction and lack of adaptability'. But I also believe it is a difficult point to sustain. Even if it were accepted, such a viewpoint must force its advocates to give increasing weight to other, mainly 'contextual' influences on Britain's economic history, so helpfully turning the argument away from the narrow focus on structure.

I want at this point to clarify some of John Quail's interpretations of my views or the emphasis he places on them. I do not, for example, 'argue the value of the holding company as a means of innovation'. Recognising the complex origins of entrepreneurial, corporate and scientific innovation, I am rather 'cowardly' in my neutrality. As my critic also states, some 'unitary joint stock companies' in Britain likewise lacked innovation. The later Schumpeter noted the links between large-scale business and expenditure on research and development. In technologically-driven industries, a multidivisional may indeed gain the synergies of centralised R&D across a portfolio of related diversification, but this consequential scenario does not affect the circumstances and cases I was generally exploring. On matters of 'organizational' innovation, British holding companies did show an ability to reorganize internally, and Chandler and others acknowledge their evolution, even if they do not fully recognise its extent. I do not know, on the other hand, how John Quail's belief that these changes represented 'the bare minimum needed for commercial survival' might be evaluated. I have to accept that it is a for many of the cases reasonable judgement, although I think there are good theoretical and empirical grounds for justifying the choice of several British holding companies. I am worried by the implicit danger of assuming an 'ideal' type to be the ultimate goal, and, taking the premise of inadequacy even further, we begin to seek explanations that are monocausal. It is no shock to state that there is evidence demonstrating managerial success and failure in specific firms; it is no shock to conclude that holding structures may have been apposite and rationale, if not a significant boon to performance. But in many cases we lack the evidence to be conclusive, and so much of what is available is open to judgement. As a result, the known record of British holding companies counsels caution against blanket condemnation of negligent or even minimal concern about strategy and governance. John Quail continues that there is a 'threshold of size, complexity and rate of change' beyond which the holding company will not suffice. My guess is that he would have welcomed the space to expand and define what he means. Depending on definition, some of these factors may indeed encourage a unitary, multidivisional form, but they may not consequently be relevant to the cases, product markets or the circumstances I was referring to (again, that is the point of the article). On different definitions, holding companies may facilitate size, complexity and change.

Quail quotes Vickers and Unilever. I am not sure why Vickers's management of the Wolseley car firm should be a particularly important test-case, but he argues that the main company should have provided the managerial resources to make Wolseley successful. That they failed to do so says much about the weakness of their organizational structure. I do not, despite the invitation, want to defend or deny the troubled record of Wolseley or Vickers in the 1920s. My lack of acquaintance with car industry records or other relevant sources adds to my personal reticence, and I am willing ultimately to concede points. Yet I want to trade Quail's reference to *Animal Farm* with the story of the dog that did not bark. As far as I know, our knowledge of the Wolseley firm from many published sources is sparse, and we do not understand enough about its management or Vickers' influence on it. According to Scott, Vickers acquired Wolseley in 1901, discerning amongst others the military potential of motorised vehicles, and only its investment matched the engineering expertise and ambitions of its new subsidiary and then manager, Herbert Austin. Although it had less than half the output of Ford, it became by 1914 Britain's second largest car maker, and its plant contributed successfully to munitions output during the first world war. The decision to re-tool Wolseley and manufacture an up-market mass-produced car appears strategically sensible in the aftermath of conflict, and suggests at least that Vickers did not neglect its subsidiary, moving as quickly as possible to re-establish its former role.[11] Yet this peace-time initiative, undertaken presumably in expectation of a growing new market, undoubtedly floundered.

Church states that both the independent Austin and Wolseley, compared to Morris, were greatly disadvantaged by their over-commitment in munitions, with plant, operational systems and short production-runs being unsuited to car manufacture. Both Austin and Wolseley were unprofitable in the difficult economic circumstances of the early 1920s. The problems and disadvantages of British car firms and their markets have been cited by various historians, and, relative to the US, help to explain differences in management, industrial structure, engineering, and employment, which were to have important longer-term consequences. With the expansive Morris, which was to purchase Wolseley, remaining an epitome of 'personal capitalism', deep managerial hierarchies in the British domestic car market were not therefore immediately pivotal. As well as forestalling a rival, Morris was motivated by an 'admirable plant', a dealer network, and the opportunity to make higher grade models. Pent-up demand and the 'newness' of the industry facilitated the entry of firms, with the more established, over-capitalised Wolseley seemingly badly-positioned to cope with the competition and high mortality rate. As the firm was unprofitable, it did not offer Vickers alternative cash flows to its interests in shipbuilding and armaments, and the peacetime benefits of 'corporate relations' within a holding company did not materialise. The decision to sell in 1926 was commercially rational, and, as an identifiable subsidiary, easily achieved. In linking a few pieces of data, I am mindful of the risks involved, but there is clearly an alternative version to a well-placed Wolseley failed by the Vickers management, or more probably to the emphasis we might place on such an account. If we were to take a more universal view of the worldwide car industry and its history, these reservations do not deny the significance of synergies and scale, the appropriateness of the multidivisional structure, nor ultimate British failure. As Church hints, these organizational lessons may not have been so evident or appropriate to the domestic car market and its industry in the 1920s.[12]

I was not oblivious to the Unilever case, and I think that Chandler misinterprets this company when he highlights characteristics he regards as failings. Like Coats, Unilever is a company that makes us hesitate before contrasting the multidivisional with the holding company or some of its variations so starkly, because structure and management may represent adjustments to each unique corporate case. From its formation in 1929, it has dealt with the tensions between strategic development and required local autonomy, and between overlapping functional, regional-national, and product responsibilities. Chandler's defenders would accommodate its organizational matrix within his overall framework, but acknowledge it is not the 'classic' multidivisional prototype revealed through General Motors, DuPont, or even ICI. The particular nature of Unilever's strategic and structural exigencies continued to be recognised by its organizational review of 1996.[13]

3. Comparisons and Japan

John Quail questions my interpretation of Japanese big business and their holding company structures, focusing on aspects he regards as more important than mere organizational form. There is, of course, a measure of illegitimacy in any comparison, especially one that is international, and I was myself eager to stress the role of context, substitute methods, and varying interactions between factors. This caveat does not, however, invalidate the lessons that are available from comparisons, and they can assist the redefinition of issues and the formation of more suitable generalizations. There were structural similarities between holding companies in the two countries, although historians accept that any gap in the quality of management between Britain and Japan was closing during the inter-war period. The export record certainly reveals a narrowing of competitiveness, most obviously in Asian markets.

I would take issue with several points and perspectives indicated by Quail. He is more concerned with the behavioural assumptions of management and their origins in national culture. Once more, I would have to accept that this is a fair approach, entrenched in a long and honourable academic tradition. The argument between 'cultural' and 'economic' explanations is complex, but possibly unanswerable, even unfruitful. I wanted, not surprisingly, to avoid this debate, because the lessons I sought to extract from an Anglo-Japanese comparison are not in essence greatly affected by the cultural dimension. In isolating the topic of structure and organization, I faced the danger of engaging in abstract analysis, but I think that this process is legitimate for comparisons seeking to define issues, and that my use of empirical evidence avoided pitfalls. I would note that the concept of 'clan', more applicable to Korea, may not be suited to Japan, where notions of the 'vertical society' have more readily been used. Moreover, Japanese business historians have already switched from the cultural traits of organization to a concern for function and their effective implementation, and I have followed this approach. I believe Quail's portrayal of the evolution of Japanese business does not take account of the many variations between companies, most notably across sectors with differing product markets, as in the example of Britain. My analysis is more vulnerable to the differences in intent and therefore consequence that flow from timing and national economic conditions, and I was only able to allude to these. I would be happy for these to be included, because they stress the external and national contexts that Chandler's comparative approach does not properly incorporate.[14]

4. Management Models and History

Among the numerous analyses of management models, the work of Grant is especially relevant because he distinguishes between the various advantages held by diversified and large-scale companies. He notes the potential of 'corporate relatedness' from which businesses can benefit in terms of risk-avoidance, commonality in decision-making and implementation, and the utilisation of core skills in strategy, finance and control. Grant is seeking to explain the rationale of unrelated diversification within conglomerates. 'Operational relatedness', on the other hand, arises from technological, operational and scale synergies, and may encourage unitary, multidivisional structures as well as related diversification. In realising these specific benefits, a company has to bear considerable costs in vertical coordination and horizontal interaction, while corporate relatedness emphasises transferable knowledge and skills. The levering of core competencies, in other words, may have alternatives in more diverse market opportunities, commercial information, and entrepreneurial initiative.[15] Kay also adds support for the conglomerate and its profitability, and he concentrates particularly on the spreading of risks. He argues that, once formed, the costs and danger of integration explain its long-term robustness and longevity.[16]

The recent book by Whittington and Mayer provides an analysis of post-war European management and argues for the superiority of the multidivisional. They, nonetheless, review the Chandlerian strategy of 'diversification and divisionalisation'. While big business structures in Britain followed those in the U.S., they note the resilience of personal management styles and holding companies in France or Germany. Whittington and Mayer contend that the 'essential' multidivisional form is currently intact and even becoming more entrenched, Europe included. But they revise theories of management, and believe that: 'The Chandlerian model of diversification should be extended to embrace the once unloved conglomerate'. By focusing on the rationale of diversification, they hold that the appropriateness of corporate relations can be incorporated. Such enterprises should no longer be viewed as evolutionary freaks, the creation of over-active financial markets, or merely the result of self-aggrandizing managerial interests. They are critical of the inability of conglomerates to ensure managerial succession 'over periods of two decades or more', though it is less clear why this should necessarily be so. They state too that their prevalence in Germany is partly explained by 'special ownership factors' and a tolerance of poor performance, a somewhat contentious view.[17]

The joint authors provide powerful support for Chandler's core thesis, and they are in spirit more supportive of John Quail's position than that of various critics. But they do acknowledge needed theoretical adjustments, and such ideas have been used to reassess the purposes and organization of large companies. I believe that historical questions about the quality of British management and its decision-making in the particular business and other circumstances that they faced are both revealing and indicative, and that this contextual, more multifaceted approach continues to be the implicit practice of historians. The specific contribution of Chandler can be built upon in the search to understand and re-assess Britain's economic and corporate past.

Notes

1 R. Fitgerald, 'The competitive and institutional advantages of holding companies: British business in the inter-war period', *Journal of Industrial History*, Vol. 3 (2000), No. 2, pp. 1–30.

2 A. D. Chandler, *Strategy and Structure: Chapters in the History of Industrial Enterprise* (Cambridge, Mass., 1962); A. D. Chandler, *The Visible Hand: the Management Revolution in American Business* (Cambridge, Mass., 1977).

3 Amongst others, R. P. Rumelt, *Strategy, Structure and Economic Performance* (Cambridge, Mass., 1974); C. C. Markides, *Diversification, Refocusing and Economic Performance* (Cambridge, Mass., 1985); D. F. Channon, *The Strategy and Structure of British Enterprise* (London, 1973); G. P. Dyas and H. T. Thanheiser, *The Emerging European Enterprise: Strategy and Structure in French and German Industry* (London, 1976); R. J. Pavan, 'Strategy and Structure: the Italian Experience', *Journal of Economics and Business*, 28, pp. 254–60.

4 A. D. Chandler, *Scale and Scope: the Dynamics of Industrial Enterprise* (Cambridge, Mass., 1990).

5 See endnotes in original article.

6 For example, M. Granovetter, 'Economic Action, Social Structure and Embeddedness', *American Journal of Sociology*, 91, pp. 481–510; R. Whitley, ed., *European Business Systems: Firms and Markets in Comparative Perspective* (London, 1992); R. Whitley, *Business Systems in East Asia: Firms, Markets and Societies* (London, 1992).

7 For example, N. Fligstein, *The Transformation of Corporate Control* (Cambridge, Mass., 1990); M. L. Djelic, *Exporting the American Model: the Post-War Transformation of European Business* (Oxford, 1998).

8 W. M. Fruin, *The Japanese Enterprise System: Competitive Strategies and Cooperative Structures* (Oxford, 1993).

9 Y. Cassis, *Big Business: the European Experience in the Twentieth Century* (Oxford, 1997).

10 R. Fitzgerald, 'Ownership, Organization, and Management: British Business and the Branded Consumer Goods Industries', in Y. Cassis, F. Crouzet and T. Gourvish, eds, *Management and Business in Britain and France: the Age of the Corporate Economy* (Oxford, 1995), pp. 31–51; R. Fitzgerald, *Rowntree and the Marketing Revolution* (Cambridge, 1995), pp. 185–216.

11 J. D. Scott, *Vickers: A History* (London, 1962), pp. 83, 140; St. J. C. Nixon, *Wolseley: a Saga of the Motor Industry* (London, 1949), pp. 18–19, 43–4, 47, 60–2, 66, 68, 71, 89–96, 157; P. L. Cook and R. Cohen, *Effects of Mergers: Six Studies* (London, 1958), pp. 359, 362–3; K. Richardson, *The British Motor Industry* (London, 1977), p. 76; G. Maxcy and A. Silbertson, eds, *The Motor Industry* (London, 1959), p. 12; M. Adeney, *Nuffield: A Biography* (London, 1993), pp. 43, 53; S. B. Saul, 'The Motor Industry in Britain to 1914', *Business History* (1962); R. Church, *Herbert Austin: the British Motor Car Industry to 1941* (London, 1979), pp. 2–3, 12, 35–6.

12 R. Church, *The Rise and Decline of the British Motor Industry* (Cambridge, 1995), pp. 9–45; W. Lewchuck, *American Technology and the British Vehicle Industry* (Cambridge, 1987), pp. 117, 119, 129, 131–184; Scott, *Vickers*, pp. 151,167; Nixon, *Wolseley*, pp. 96, 99–100, 103, 154, 157; Cook and Cohen, *Effects of Mergers*, p. 367; Richardson, *British Motor Industry*, pp. 79, 82; R. J. Overy, *William Morris, Viscount Nuffield* (London, 1976), pp. 28, 30, 34, 40, 55, 73; Church, *Herbert Austin*, pp. 53, 105, 179, 186–7, 191, 196; P. W. S. Andrews and E. Brunner, *The Life of Lord Nuffield: A Study in Enterprise and Benevolence* (Oxford, 1955), pp. 154, 156–7.

13 A. D. Bonham-Carter, 'Centralisation and Decentralisation in Unilever', in R. S. Edwards and H. Townsend, ed., *Business Enterprise: its Growth and Organisation* (London, 1961); C. Wilson, *Unilever, 1945–1965: Challenge and Response in the Post-War Industrial Revolution* (London, 1968), pp. 29–41; Chandler, *Scale and Scope*, pp. 378–89; R. Whittington and M. Mayer, *The European Corporation: Strategy, Structure and Social Science* (Oxford, 2000), pp. 177–87.

14 I am indebted to Professor Nobuo Kawabe for helping me to clarify my thoughts on these issues (without suggesting he is responsible for my views).

15 R. M. Grant, 'On Dominant Logic, Relatedness and the Link between Diversity and Performance', *Strategic Management* Journal, vol. 9 (1988), pp. 639–42.

16 N. M. Kay, *Patterns in Corporate Development* (Oxford, 1997).

17 Whittington and Mayer, *European Corporation*.

Retrospective

Large Firms, Organizational Structures and Comparisons within Business History

Robert Fitzgerald

Recalling your motives for an article written so long ago is a challenge: 'Corporate Structures and Holding Companies in Britain: Evidence, Comparison and Appraisal' appeared in 2002. In so far as I remember accurately, I was merely joining many business historians distancing themselves from Chandler's dominating paradigm, searching for other approaches and insights. Ultimately, because I was still attempting to debate big business organization, that aim was only partially successful.

Appearing in 1990, *Scale and Scope* extended Chandler's previous arguments about the success of large 20th century U.S. companies resting on coordinating managerial hierarchies, multidivisional structures, and returns to scale. In his comparison of the U.S., Britain and Germany, he identified their relative economic performance with the adherence of their biggest firms to the principles of managerial enterprise. Chandler argued that Cadbury Brothers was an archetypal example of how British firms remained family managed and, as a result, devoid of the professionalized systems that could safeguarded its commercial growth. From my work on the confectionery industry, I already knew that Chandler had spectacularly misunderstood this business, which proved conclusively that a family-managed firm could be highly professionalized and competitive. The other line of attack on Britain was that its holding companies were simply oligopolistic federations to maintain family control, and so prevented industrial and managerial reorganization.

The difficulty was that holding companies were notable in 'successful' Germany and Japan before the Second World War, while, unconvincingly, 'unsuccessful' Britain had all the bad types. Chandler's comparative method exaggerated the differences between economies, while, eager to see patterns within each national case, he underestimated variations in the management of large firms. Holding companies and business groups potentially offered a range of advantages in operational flexibility, cash flow, capital financing, costs, labour skills, customization, marketing, product and brand retention,

DOI: 10.4324/9781003313397-5

vertical integration, and scope economies. They could be well-suited to particular economies or industries.

On formation, British holding companies in textiles, engineering and shipbuilding often had many of the managerial and operational deficiencies Chandler cites, but he seems unaware of later developments that, if not fitting the 'required' trajectory of integrated managerial enterprises, they nevertheless had strategic rationale. The companies became better, over time, at building a headquarters function when change could be advantageous (such as overseeing finance and accounting, or establishing new businesses or overseas subsidiaries), and also at merging duplicated operations. But they might maintain operational diversity and inherited firms to manage batch manufacturing or legacy brands. Restructuring and managerial reorganisation, therefore, did occur: unsurprisingly, the initiatives were not always sufficient, but even the most comprehensive internal reforms were not necessarily the answer to the huge problems these businesses faced in the inter-war decades. In Japan, finally not included in *Scale and Scope*, the *zaibatsu* led the process of industrialization, despite being family-controlled holding companies. In the article, they served as a useful comparator to draw more balanced lessons about British holding companies in the inter-war period. As well as attempting to move debates away from 'one best way' to organize large enterprises in all circumstances, it was important to question if managerial organization was such an important factor in the success or failure of firms.

I cannot help, in a retrospective vein, regretting that the critique in the article was far too restrained. Leslie Hannah, in particular, has forcefully challenged the credibility of the Chandler thesis by questioning its methods and use of evidence. Moreover, by 2002, we already had interesting historical lessons about the strategies and organization of trading firms. After that date, research has emphasized the vital role of holding companies and business groups within emerging economies, and their political and institutional implications. We have gained insights into the strategic value of networks, geographic clusters and other 'externalities', which Chandler's focus on internal organization ignores, and reflected on what they say about the nature and significance of market mechanisms. Transnational corporations in the 21st century have evolved increasingly complex ownership, managerial and contractual relationships that utilize alliances, joint ventures, and informal association alongside integration and control. The theory of managerial enterprise still offers useful lessons. Business history just seems more complicated, and its insights less straightforward. But, in investigating the dynamic between firms, organizations, their contexts, and long-term development, it has grown in depth and richness.

Robert Fitzgerald
Royal Holloway, University of London
12.01.2021

4 The Tank Producers

British Mechanical Engineering in the Great War

John Singleton

Tanks were first sent into action by the British army at Flers on the Somme on 15 September 1916.[1] This was a revolutionary episode in the history of military technology. Tanks played a key part in the attack at Cambrai in 1917, and were prominent at the battles of Hamel and Amiens in 1918.[2] During the winter of 1917–18, the British believed that the war was unlikely to be won in 1918, and plans were drawn up to create a mechanical army for the 1919 fighting season. Winston Churchill, who was Minister of Munitions in 1917–18, hoped for the production of 10,000 tanks per annum (4,500 in Britain and the rest, under a joint programme with the Americans, in France). Churchill's plans were extremely optimistic but, if the war had continued, it is conceivable that the tank would have become the decisive weapon in land warfare in 1919, instead of in 1939.

Although there are accounts of the British coal, steel, and chemical industries during the Great War, and histories of individual armaments companies, there is no modern literature on the manufacture of particular weapons at the national level.[3] The central purpose of this article is to discuss the establishment and coordination of an extensive network of engineering and steel firms for the production of tanks. Britain's often maligned engineering industry manufactured 2,619 tanks between 1915 and 1918, and it was gearing up for even greater efforts in 1919. Given that the tank was a new invention, it is difficult to devise an objective measure of the success of the tank programme. But it was to the credit of an essentially Victorian industry that several thousand of these strange machines were built at short notice. Tanks were by no means an engineering marvel, but they did incorporate some technical improvements, especially in the area of caterpillar mechanisms, and their manufacture required the recombination of existing types of components into a new end product.

Traditional armaments manufacturers assembled relatively few tanks. Most tanks were built by producers of railway equipment or agricultural machinery. Assemblers had to be supplied with armour plate, internal

DOI: 10.4324/9781003313397-6

combustion engines, caterpillar mechanisms, weaponry, and a myriad of other components. The tank production network cut across established demarcations in the metal goods sector. This network was forged by government orders, and supervised by government officials. Comparable networks were developed for the production of other munitions, such as aeroplanes, but historians have neglected them as well. Wartime production networks did not endure after 1918 – the tank had no commercial uses. But many of the firms in the tank programme did benefit from the acquisition of new engineering skills. The tank programme was a monument to what could be achieved in a crisis by the engineering industry, but it offered few pointers to the future.

The first section outlines the military and administrative context of the tank programme. The growth of the tank complex is discussed in the second section. Production bottlenecks are examined in the third section. The aftermath of the war for the tank producers is considered in the fourth section.

1

Tanks came in two basic designs. 'Heavy' tanks (Mk I to Mk VIII) were employed to attack fixed positions in cooperation with infantry and artillery.[4] Faster 'medium' tanks were supposed to help the cavalry to exploit any breakthrough in the enemy's trench system.[5] Most tanks built during the war were of the heavy variety. An initial order for 100 tanks was placed at the start of 1916, but tank production did not begin in earnest until 1917 (see Table 4.1). Despite a rising trend, there was no prospect of the British tank factories reaching Churchill's ambitious output target of 4,339 machines between February 1918 and March 1919.[6,7]

The armed forces and the government never questioned the importance of ships, aeroplanes, artillery, and shells. As a new invention, however, the tank had to prove itself in the field, and it did not immediately win universal acclaim.[8] One of the most powerful arguments in favour of tanks was an economic one – tanks could save thousands of lives by substituting for masses of infantry during an attack.[9] But their early performance on the Somme, where they were sent into quagmires, was disappointing. Critics, including the German high command, regarded the tank as a gimmick, and this uncertainty about its military value was a handicap in the scrabble for inputs, particularly in the early stages of the programme.

A body consecutively known as the Tank Supply Committee, Tank Supply Department, Mechanical Warfare Supply Department, and Mechanical Warfare Department (MWD) planned the tank programme, arranged for the distribution of orders among suppliers, inspected components and

Table 4.1 British tank output, 1916–1918[a]

	1916	1917	1918	Total
Heavy Fighting Machines				
Mark I	150	–	–	150
Marks II and III	–	100	–	100
Mark IV	–	910	105	1015
Mark V	–	–	400	400
Mark V*	–	–	632	632
MarkV**	–	–	1	1
Mark VII	–	–	–	_b
Mark VIII (Liberty)	–	–	1	1
Light or Chaser Tanks				
Medium A (Whippet)	–	55	145	200
Medium B	–	–	45	45
Medium C	–	–	–	_b
Supply and Miscellaneous Machines				
Gun Carriers and Salvage Tanks	–	45	5	50
Infantry Supply Tanks (Mark IX)	–	–	25	25
GRAND TOTAL	150	1110	1359	2619

Source: *History of the Ministry of Munitions* (London, 1921), vol. XII, part III, p. 93.
[a] Deliveries down to 31 Dec. 1918, exclusive of fighting machines converted as supply tanks.
[b] Formal delivery of first machine was made in Jan. 1919

finished tanks, and liaised with the manufacturers.[10] The MWD was answerable to the Munitions Council. A. G. Stern, a banker, Admiral Moore, and J. B. Maclean, the former head of engineering at the Ministry of Munitions, were the successive Controllers of the MWD. These men were not experts in industrial coordination and they needed help in this sphere. In early 1917, Stern asked Percival Perry, managing director of The Ford Company (Europe) Ltd, to advise the MWD. Perry later became Deputy Controller, and his manufacturing experience proved invaluable. He advocated the decentralization of the MWD's activities. Regional offices were duly established in the main centres of production.[11]

Table 4.2 outlines the material requirements of the Mk V heavy tank and the Medium B tank. Tank production was not a large consumer of steel in comparison with shipbuilding and shell manufacturing. Under the munitions programme, drawn up in November 1917, the Admiralty (which always had priority) was to receive twenty times as much steel as the tank factories. It was reckoned that tanks would need less than two per cent of the steel allocated to the munitions programme.[12] Although the use of steel in tanks clearly did not threaten the shipbuilding and shell programmes, there were intense disputes over the allocation of steel at the margin. Tank production was extremely vulnerable to relatively small changes in the steel allocations. It was fortunate that Churchill, as First Lord of the Admiralty,

Table 4.2 *Material requirements for tank production, 1918 (tons)*

	100 Mark Vs	100 Medium Bs
Armour plate	1100	550
Steel	1930	1161
Steel alloy	100	75
Cast iron	170	50
Copper	22	15
Yellow metal	38	25
Aluminium	5	4

Source: *History of the Ministry of Munitions* (London, 1921), vol. XII, part III, p. 58.

and later as Minister of Munitions, was a great tank enthusiast. In 1917–18, Churchill fought hard against the Admiralty to ensure that the tank programme was not sacrificed to meet the insatiable demands of shipbuilding, and he eventually gained permission to use more steel in the tank works.[13]

When forced to choose, the army consistently expressed a preference for aeroplanes over tanks. This reflected the fact that aeroplanes were essential for observing activity behind enemy lines and artillery spotting. Aeroplanes were made from wood and fabric at this early stage, but there was severe competition between the aeroplane and tank programmes over engine supplies. In early 1917, the commander of the British Expeditionary Force, Douglas Haig, made it plain that, whilst it was important to produce more tank engines, there was an even greater need for aero-engines and engines for light railway locomotives.[14] Britain's limited output of internal combustion engines had to be shared among the makers of tanks, mechanical transport (or lorries), light railway locomotives, and aeroplanes. Although aeroplanes and tanks required engines made to different specifications, they utilized the same production skills.[15] In August 1917, engines were being produced in the ratio of nine for the aeroplane for every one for the tank programme.[16] The supply of tank engines rose in the final year of the war, but it remained a troublesome bottleneck. Not until almost the end of the war did tanks achieve priority over aeroplanes.[17]

Tank producers were embroiled in a chronic struggle for labour supplies in wartime Britain. Whereas the state exercised a fair degree of control over the allocation of steel, coal, and other basic inputs, it had no power to determine the industrial distribution of the labour force.[18] Factories producing tanks had to compete for labour on the open market. A heavy tank cost 20,000 hours of labour, and a medium tank 16,000 hours.[19] The government was as helpful as it could be under the circumstances. It delayed the conscription of tank workers, and directed some troops to work in the tank factories. A procedure was introduced in 1916 to identify 'T' men, who would be of greater use in the tank factories than in the trenches.[20]

But, in times of military crisis, such as the German offensive of 1918, even key tank workers had to be sent to the front, and production suffered as a result. In October 1918, the leading tank manufacturers estimated that their stocks of labour still were one-third below the level required to meet construction targets.[21]

Admittedly, the tank programme was not at the centre of the war effort between 1915 and 1918, but its claims on resources would have grown rapidly in 1919 if the war had not finished. The MWD, the tank assemblers, and their suppliers had to manage on the scraps which Churchill extracted from the shipbuilding, shell, and aeroplane programmes. They operated in a difficult environment, and their achievements must be judged accordingly.

2

A network of 4,000 contractors and subcontractors, encompassing most of industrial Britain, from Kent to Tayside, underpinned the 1918–19 tank programme.[22] The members of this complex were drawn from both the traditional and the modern halves of the engineering industry (see Table 4.3). This section discusses the formation and management of the tank production network.

Railway locomotives, rolling stock, steam engines, agricultural machinery, armaments, textile machinery, and heavy machine tools were the core products of the British engineering industry. On the eve of the Great War, Britain also possessed significant productive capacity in the newer branches of engineering, such as the manufacture of motor vehicles, bicycles, and electrical machinery. The attempts of economic historians to assess the health of the engineering industry, in the early twentieth century, have been hampered by this sector's diversity. Ground was certainly being lost in established export lines, to American and German competitors, before 1914. But it was not until after the Great War that the older mechanical engineering firms ran into serious difficulties: demand for their products stagnated, and foreign competitors showed greater initiative in productive techniques, marketing, and diversification.[23] The wartime experience of firms in the traditional sections of British engineering did not result in any sustained improvement in performance.

It is generally believed that, after some teething troubles, British manufacturing industry gave a more than satisfactory account of itself between 1915 and 1918. Output barely fell, despite the fact that millions of men joined the armed forces. State intervention in the munitions industry was reasonably successful.[24] This article does not dissent from the received view of the war effort. The tank programme demonstrated that British mechanical engineers did not lack either flexibility or ingenuity, at least when they were

Table 4.3 Principal firms involved in the tank programme, 1915–18

	Principal line of business	Location of tank work
Tank assemblers		
MCWF	Rolling stock	Birmingham
W. Foster & Co.	Agricultural machinery	Lincoln
Armstrong Whitworth	Armaments	Newcastle
W. Beardmore & Co.	Armaments	Glasgow
Brown Brothers	Engineering	Edinburgh
Coventry Ordnance Works	Armaments	Glasgow
Kitson & Co.	Locomotives	Leeds
Marshall Sons & Co.	Agricultural machinery	Gainsborough
North British Loco. Co.	Locomotives	Glasgow
Armour suppliers		
Edgar Allen & Co.	Steel	Sheffield
W. Beardmores & Co.	Armaments	Glasgow
Cammell Laird	Armaments	Sheffield
D. Colville & Co.	Steel	Motherwell
Steel Co. of Scotland	Steel	Glasgow
Vickers	Armaments	Sheffield
Engine manufacturers		
Peter Brotherhood	Engineering	Peterborough
Browett, Lindley & Sons	Steam engines	Manchester
Crossley Brothers	Internal combustion engines	Manchester
Daimler	Motor vehicles	Coventry
L. Gardner & Co.	Internal combustion engines	Manchester
Perkins Engineers	Baking machinery	Peterborough
Tilling Stevens	Motor omnibuses	Maidstone
Gearing and transmission		
J. Fowler & Co.	Agricultural machinery	Leeds
Halleys Industrial Motors	Motor vehicle components	Glasgow
Mather & Platt	Textile machinery	Manchester
Rover Motor Co.	Motor vehicles	Coventry
Star Engineering	Motor vehicle components	Wolverhampton
Tilling Stevens	Motor omnibuses	Maidstone
E. G. Wrigley & Co.	Motor vehicle components	Birmingham
Caterpillar track		
Coventry Chain Co.	Chains	Coventry
Hans Renold	Chains	Manchester
J. Fowler & Co.	Agricultural machinery	Leeds
Sir Robert Hadfield	Armaments	Sheffield
Robert Hyde & Son	Steel	Sheffield
T. & T. Vicars	Biscuit machinery	Earlestown

Source: PRO, MUN4/5204, List of Labour Requirements of Tank Producers, 11 Oct. 1918. I have used this list of firms as a guide.

Note: Except for the list of assemblers, this table must not be taken as definitive, due to the constraints of space, and the incomplete nature of the evidence.

supervised by a government department, and freed of the need to compete in export markets.

A decision was taken, in December 1915, to put the successful prototype tank into production as the Mk I.[25] Lincoln and Birmingham were the earliest locations for tank assembly. Lincoln's involvement in the tank programme was a product of its expertise in the manufacture of agricultural machinery.[26] William Foster & Son of Lincoln were awarded a contract in 1914–15, to make wheeled tractors for the heavy howitzers, which were being manufactured by the Coventry Ordnance Works (COW). Reginald Bacon, the managing director of the COW, suggested that Fosters should also participate in experimental work on an armoured tractor. During 1915, Fosters and their managing director, William Tritton, were active in the experimental tank programme, in collaboration with technical experts from the armed forces, including Walter Wilson, a former designer of motor vehicles. Tritton and Wilson were the key figures in the design of the early tanks. One of the main challenges was the inadequacy of the available caterpillar mechanisms. But Fosters were experienced in the manufacture of agricultural caterpillar tractors, and Tritton invented an improved type of caterpillar track for the prototype tank. But Fosters, however, lacked the productive capacity to become a volume supplier of tanks. It would be necessary to bring a larger assembler into the programme, once a machine was ready to go into production. An obvious choice was Dudley Docker's Metropolitan Carriage, Wagon & Finance (MCWF), one of Britain's largest producers of rolling stock. MCWF had large factories at Saltley and Oldbury, near Birmingham. This firm had taken part in the experimental tank programme, if only briefly, and it clearly had the potential to become a mass supplier of armoured fighting vehicles. When orders were placed for the Mk I, they were in the ratio of three tanks from MCWF to every one from Fosters.[27]

No firm could have produced an entire tank from scratch. The tank was a hybrid: part motor vehicle, part miniature warship. The main elements were a chassis, powerful internal combustion engines, a body made from armour plate, two caterpillar tracks, and a complement of small naval guns and machine guns. The MWD undertook to arrange for the delivery of armour plate, engines, and weaponry to the assemblers; hence the government was responsible for the establishment of the core network of suppliers. At first, assemblers were left to make their own arrangements with subcontractors for deliveries of other components, such as caterpillar tracks, gearboxes, and steel castings. But this procedure threatened to lead to an unseemly scramble for supplies, particularly as new assemblers were brought into the programme. Manufacture of some of these components was also blighted by poor quality control. Consequently, in 1917, the MWD assumed responsibility for organizing their supply to the assembly plants.[28]

The tank programme grew rapidly during 1917 and 1918, and the MWD recruited and trained many additional component suppliers. For instance, it took an average of six months for a new producer of tracks to reach an acceptable quality of work.[29] Many famous companies contributed to the tank programme. Armstrong Whitworth's plant at Elswick, Newcastle, supplied the overwhelming number of 6-pder naval guns employed in tanks. This was a standard type of light naval gun. Towards the end of the war, Beardmores also began to produce guns for tanks.[30] Armour plate for the first batch of tanks was ordered from Vickers, Cammell Laird, and Beardmores. These companies were among the major producers of armour for the navy.[31] Other suppliers of tank armour included the Steel Company of Scotland, Colvilles, and Edgar Allen.[32] Hardly surprisingly, the pressure of naval work led to frequent delays in the delivery of tank armour. It was fortunate, therefore, that MCWF had its own steel works at Wednesbury which could supply Saltley and Oldbury in an emergency.[33]

The 105 h.p. engines used in the original 1916 tanks were supplied by Daimler. This Coventry firm had made the engine for Fosters' howitzer tractor, and it worked closely with Fosters on the modification of this engine for use in tanks. Unfortunately, conditions on the Somme were such that the first tanks became literally stuck in the mud, and Daimler failed to deliver a more powerful engine. In October 1916, a different engine, developed by Harry Ricardo, was adopted by the MWD, and variants of this type became the standard in heavy tanks for the remainder of the war.[34] The Ricardo engines for the tank programme were made by a number of firms, including Peter Brotherhood, Browett, Lindley & Sons, Crossleys, and Gardners, and there were plans, in 1918–19, to extend production to such enterprises as the National Gas Engine Company of Ashton-under-Lyne, and British Westinghouse of Trafford Park, Manchester.[35] Other firms, including Tilling Stevens and Perkins specialized in building engines for medium tanks. Although experienced manufacturers of internal combustion engines, such as Crossleys and Gardners, were the principal suppliers of tank engines, it is interesting that the MWD was prepared to admit a maker of baking machinery, Perkins, into the programme. This reflected desperation on the part of the MWD, an urgent need for work on the part of Perkins, and a shared belief in the adaptability of skilled engineering personnel.[36]

Suppliers of gearing and tracks were crucial to the tank programme. Among the makers of tank gearing were Fowlers, Halleys, Mather & Platt, Star Engineering, Tilling Stevens, and Wrigleys.[37] Hans Renold and Coventry Chain, firms with wide experience in the manufacture of chains for bicycles and industrial purposes, were the earliest suppliers of tracks. As the tank programme expanded, Hans Renold and Coventry Chain trained other companies to make these vital components. The mentoring of inexperienced firms by established producers was one way in which information and know-how could be disseminated through the network. By the end of the war, firms such as Hadfields, Robert Hyde & Son, and T. & T. Vicars (another manufacturer of baking machinery), were supplying tracks or parts of tracks to the MWD.[38] Special steel was needed in track manufacture and, in 1918, Cammell Laird installed a three ton electric furnace for this purpose.[39] Ball-bearings were another essential ingredient in tanks, aeroplanes and mechanical transport. Each tank required 300 ball-bearings. Germany had met a large proportion of British needs before the war. Only six British factories made ball-bearing parts in 1914, and only one manufactured whole ball-bearing assemblies. But domestic production expanded, between 1914 and 1918, as extensions were made to these firms. Electric Ordnance & Accessories, of Birmingham, made a particularly important contribution to the tank programme by overcoming a bottleneck in the supply of Timken bearings.[40]

Numerous firms were involved in other aspects of the tank programme, and it is not possible to mention more than a few of them. The Leeds Forge Company supplied jigs for tank assembly.[41] Heenan & Froude (Manchester), West's Gas Improvement Company (Manchester), Hurst Nelson (Kilmarnock), and Mechans (Glasgow) supplied hulls.[42] GEC made electric fans.[43] Gardners were responsible for the entire production of crankshafts used in tank engines, and they designed their own machine tools for this work.[44]

In the winter of 1916–17 it became clear that the projected growth in tank numbers would require the introduction of extra assemblers. Enquiries were made throughout the country to find suitable capacity.[45] Armstrong Whitworth received a small order for Mk IVs; Marshalls were asked to manufacture supply tanks; the COW was invited to produce Medium B tanks; Kitsons were put under contract to supply gun carrier tanks; and Brown Brothers were given an order to assemble Mk VIIs.[46] In 1918, the North British Locomotive Company and Beardmores were also recruited as tank assemblers. Beardmores managed the government's National Projectile Factory at Cardonald, and offered to produce tanks in the idle portion of this shell works.[47] Although most of the above firms were given small orders, it was intended that North British should manufacture tanks in bulk in 1919. In June 1918, tanks were on order from the following companies: MCWF (2180 machines); North British (1140); Fosters (700); Beardmores (335); Patent Shaft & Axletree (250); Marshalls (200); the COW (100); Kitsons (36); and Brown Brothers (28).[48] Many of these machines were destined never to be built. After the Armistice the bulk of the outstanding orders was cancelled.[49]

As demand for tanks grew, the MWD attempted to develop regional tank production networks, so that it could make use of spare industrial capacity wherever it could be found.[50] Scotland was scheduled to be the next most important region (after the English Midlands). Lancashire and Yorkshire would also be developed into important centres of tank-related production.

Regional tank committees were set up in Glasgow, Manchester, and Leeds.[51] North British, the COW, and Beardmores were the core members of the tank group in Glasgow. Kitsons were at the centre of the somewhat limited Yorkshire tank programme. Engine producers, such as Crossleys and Gardners, were more prominent in Lancashire, although the chairman of the Manchester Tank Committee represented the supplier of tank hulls, West's Gas Improvement Company.[52] Businessmen on these committees worked with the regional officers of the MWD to coordinate the supply of components and labour, and to find solutions to bottlenecks.[53] These regional networks were conduits for the dissemination of information about technical developments and production methods among member firms. While the regional tank programmes were not expected to be self-contained, the ministry did hope that they would obtain most of their inputs locally. The Scottish group, for instance, faced a large deficit in engines; and the mission of the Manchester group was not to produce complete machines, but rather to make engines for other regions, and to supply hulls and other components to the proposed Anglo-American tank factory in France.[54]

Between 1915 and 1918, an extensive network of firms was created to satisfy the burgeoning demands of the tank programme. The government was responsible for the vetting of assemblers and component suppliers. This was inevitable, in view of the need for haste, and the fact that industry had no experience in tank production. MWD officials simply had to re-wire parts of the engineering industry. Information and intermediate products were channelled in new directions, and the result was a stream of tanks for the front.

3

Many contradictions and bottlenecks had to be overcome by the tank production network, so that it could provide the army with a supply of serviceable tanks. Some of these problems reflected the strains of the wartime economy; some were the result of the immaturity of the tank as a weapon system; and yet others were the result of the obstructiveness or incompetence of MWD officials, businessmen and workers. This section identifies a number of frictions in the operation of the tank programme, and discusses how they were managed.

Several of the problems encountered by the tank producers stemmed from the behaviour of their monopsonistic customer. Internal disputes among government departments were commonplace. Communications between the MWD and the army left something to be desired. For instance, the MWD did not anticipate that damaged tanks could be repaired, and failed to provide the army with adequate supplies of spare parts. Urgent and unanticipated requests for spares held up work on the completion of new machines in 1916.[55] Churchill, on several occasions, gained approval for increases in the tank programme, without bothering to ascertain whether there was sufficient capacity to produce the requisite armour plate, steel castings, engines, and gear boxes.[56] No doubt sudden changes in output targets were unavoidable in wartime, but they added to the practical difficulties faced by the manufacturers.

Friction was also caused by the rapid succession of new models, incorporating improvements in engines, gearing, and armour. In his study of aeroplane production during the Second World War, Ely Devons discussed comparable problems. Machine tools had to be adjusted, and factory layouts had to be changed, during the transition from one type of aeroplane to another, and time and output were lost in the process.[57] The same was true for tanks in the Great War. For instance, the timing of the supersession of the Mk IV tank became a matter of dispute. In the late summer of 1917, the army wanted to cancel further deliveries of the Mk IV, and to bring forward production of a more advanced machine. But neither MCWF nor its suppliers were ready to produce the Mk V, and the MWD argued that, for the time being, it would be better to persevere with manufacture of the Mk IV. Any attempt to change over to production of the Mk V, before MCWF and the other suppliers were ready, would have slowed down deliveries to a trickle. It was better to have a steady flow of technically obsolete, but still effective, Mk IVs, than it was to have an uncertain output of the technically more advanced model. In the event, a compromise was reached, whereby some of the unwanted Mk IVs were converted into supply tanks, and others were cancelled. Production of the Mk V began in January 1918.[58]

Bottlenecks in the supply of armour plate, steel castings, gearboxes, machine tools, engines, ball bearings, coal, and labour were all, at various times, limiting factors on production. For example, shortages of structural steel threatened to halt the building of additional capacity to make the guns and machine guns needed by the tank programme.[59] MCWF's production of the Mk V was hampered, in early 1918, by late deliveries of armour plate, resulting from the shortage of heat treatment plant.[60] The priority assigned to the production of armour plate for shipbuilding was particularly detrimental to the Scottish tank programme. During 1918, Scottish tank production was held up by the inability of Beardmores to supply North British with armour plate. In the final weeks of the war, plate orders were given to Colvilles, in order to ease this bottleneck and to provide Beardmores with competition.[61] Beardmores were not wholly to blame for this crisis; they were large suppliers of armour plate to the Admiralty, a department enjoying priority over the MWD.[62]

Continuing and acute difficulties were experienced with supplies of forgings and small castings for the production of tracks, gearboxes, and engines. In the first half of 1917, up to 40 per cent of castings made for the tank programme were rejected by the MWD as substandard. To compound matters, the assemblers of tanks and caterpillar tractors were in competition for tracks.[63] High quality gearboxes were difficult to obtain throughout the war.[64] Production of the Mk V was held up until new epicyclic gearboxes were available in January 1918. Competition for gearboxes from the mechanical transport programme contributed to tardy delivery. Fosters also complained about the poor quality of the few gearboxes that it was receiving. Since gearboxes contained parts made by a number of firms, it was not easy to guarantee their uniform quality. Locomotive builders and manufacturers of printing machinery were pressed into service as makers of gears and gearboxes. Their occasionally fruitless struggles to produce work of a reasonable quality were understandable. In June 1918, Fosters argued that a lack of gearboxes was the main constraint on tank production at Lincoln. Given these difficulties, Churchill was anxious to obtain tank gearboxes from the United States, although it appeared that the Americans would not be able to commence delivery until 1919.[65] A shortage of ball-bearings was an additional headache for the tank producers.[66] As for machine tools, not only were they in short supply, but Percival Perry expressed dissatisfaction with the quality of those which were allocated to tank production. However, the machine tool issue was not as urgent as either the armour plate or the gearbox crises.

The hopes of tank assemblers for the prompt delivery of engines were often disappointed. Engine production should have risen in line with the tank programme. But it was far easier to find spare capacity for tank erection (at a pinch any large engineering works would do) than it was to secure an increase in the output of a sophisticated piece of machinery like the internal combustion engine. Until virtually the end of the war, the production of engines for aeroplanes was given priority over the production of engines for tanks. This led to an uneven rate of engine delivery to the tank assemblers, who were treated as residual customers. Engine supply was also held up for other reasons. Work on the development of 225 and 300 h.p. tank engines, in 1917–18, interfered with the delivery of existing types. American engines were ordered but failed to materialize. The shortage of engines persisted until the end the war. In October 1918, tank assembly at North British was delayed by a simultaneous lack of engines and armour.[67]

Labour shortages, and sometimes unrest, constrained production, especially in the later stages of the war. Competition for the services of highly skilled workers was intense. One MWD memorandum highlighted the 'complete dearth of draughtsmen. They have no Union and, in consequence, have not been protected from the Recruiting Sergeant. If the Army wants Tanks, draughtsmen must be released'.[68] Complaints from firms about shortages of labour were legion, and a few illustrations must suffice. Hans Renold informed the MWD, in October 1918, that a worsening labour shortage was jeopardizing the output of caterpillar tracks. If the war had continued, without the resolution of this bottleneck, the dearth of tracks would have had a serious effect on tank output.[69] At Brown Brothers' tank assembly plant in Edinburgh, an attempt was made to overcome the labour shortage by employing Danish migrants, but a strike by native Scots brought this experiment to an end.[70]

At a June 1918 conference, attended by tank contractors and ministry officials, and chaired by Churchill, representatives of the firms were asked to account for their failure to meet production targets. MCWF had completed no more than 120 tanks in June, out of a target of 260. Docker argued that, during the recent German offensive, MCWF had been hurt by the recall to the colours of a number of skilled workers, and the call up of new drafts of men. But not all firms felt that labour was the effective constraint on production. North British stated that its tank assemblers were underemployed, due to the lack of jigs and materials, and that workers were starting to drift away to better jobs.[71] Wartime conditions created a mixture of labour shortage and labour surplus.

It cannot be denied that many firms exaggerated their labour deficit, in the hope that they would receive special treatment from the recruiting sergeant. In early 1917, officials described as 'purely fictitious' MCWF's purported shortfall of 1,000 tank assembly workers.[72] Some firms were reluctant to introduce labour dilution, due to fear of provoking resistance, and this factor aggravated the overall shortage of labour. Churchill and his civil servants were not convinced by Docker's explanation of MCWF's lagging output in the summer of 1918. They felt that MCWF could have coped with the loss of skilled workers, during the second quarter of the year, if a more vigorous policy of labour dilution had been implemented. Similarly, complaints of an acute labour shortage at Crossleys were dismissed, on the grounds that, in view of union hostility, this firm had not introduced an appropriate measure of dilution.[73] The fact that a neighbouring firm, Gardners, did secure a high degree of dilution without offending the unions, suggests that the quality of labour relations was a relevant factor.[74]

Individual firms had to strike a balance between the production of tanks and other munitions. Long delays were experienced in obtaining tanks from Armstrong Whitworth. However, this firm was overloaded with orders for various types of munitions, including the bulk of the 6-pder guns for the British tank programme.[75] Wartime production could be diverse. Between 1914 and 1918, Marshalls made naval gun mountings, shells, shell fuses, military vehicles, boilers, chemical and engineering plant, and traction engines, as well as tanks.[76]

Makers of railway equipment had lost their export markets for the duration, and needed tank and other munitions orders to keep their factories occupied. But not even these firms had unlimited capacity for tank erection. The British military railway authorities in France and Belgium placed substantial orders for locomotives and rolling stock, and expected firms to meet tight delivery schedules.[77] North British first offered its services as a tank erector during a period of weak demand for locomotives. This company argued that the construction of tanks would not interfere with locomotive building. The railway authorities dissented from this optimistic prediction. Given the growing shortages of labour and machine tools, the dismay of the Railway Materials Department (RMD) was not unreasonable. Battle was also joined by the MWD and the RMD for the services of Kitsons' locomotive works at Leeds. RMD officials, who were still smarting over MCWF's role in the tank programme, were strongly opposed to the use of Kitsons for tank assembly. In the event Kitsons were allowed to produce some tanks, although they did not become major suppliers.[78]

All of these problems required careful managing. MWD officials and inspectors sought out bottlenecks and poor quality work at the factories and regional depots. Conferences of MWD officials and employers were held, at both the regional and national levels, to consider the more pervasive and urgent bottlenecks. But coordination problems were in general dealt with on an *ad hoc* basis, by contact between upstream and downstream producers, with the MWD often acting as an intermediary. Scottish tank producers experienced major difficulties, late in 1918, but there is no reason to believe that these would not have been resolved, or at least contained, if the war had continued. The tank complex was not overwhelmed by its problems; indeed the assemblers and their suppliers demonstrated a remarkable capacity for improvisation.

4

It remains to be seen whether or not participation in the tank programme bestowed any lasting benefits upon British engineering firms, and especially upon the suppliers of traditional engineering products.

The lessons of the war for the engineering sector were discussed in a report, published in 1918, by a Board of Trade committee, chaired by the overseas railway constructor, Charles Hyde. This committee lamented that a 'system of exclusiveness and aloofness marked the Engineering Trade before the war'. British manufacturers had refused to cooperate with one another, unlike their rivals in Germany and the United States. Wartime conditions had, however, encouraged a 'considerable movement towards standardising patterns, the specialisation of output, the co-ordination of production and towards the communication to each other by hitherto rival manufacturers of improved processes and methods'.[79] Hyde's committee concluded that these organizational skills would be equally necessary after the war, if British engineering companies were to maintain their place in international markets.[80]

The Hyde committee's assessment was not entirely realistic on several scores. First, the committee did not fully understand the basis of competitiveness in many branches of the engineering trade. Although there was more cooperation among German than there was among British engineering firms, with respect to cartels and information sharing agreements, this was not necessarily the source of the Germans' competitive advantage. Chandler suggests that firms in the German capital goods sector were competitive because they were larger, better managed, and more diversified than their British rivals. He also points out that customization rather than standardization was still the key to success in industries such as locomotive building.[81] There was, however, more scope for standardization in such lines as agricultural machinery, and in the manufacture of components for motor vehicles. The diversity of the engineering sector meant that there was no universally appropriate strategy.

Secondly, there was no reason to believe that emergency networks of armaments producers would possess any relevance after the war. Companies from a wide range of engineering and related trades had been brought together in the tank programme. An ethos of patriotic determination to win the war pervaded this network,[82] and members developed a sense of solidarity in the face of the perceived shortcomings of their monopsonistic final customer. Tank suppliers found plenty to grouse about. For instance, they were expected to start work on orders before the authorities had given them a price. Reginald Bacon, who had left the COW to return to the navy, and subsequently Whitehall, was sympathetic towards those tank contractors who believed that the government was a 'corporation without a conscience'.[83] But cooperation between firms had no more than a slim chance of surviving the armistice, and the withdrawal of the government from supervision of the engineering trade. Wartime collaboration would not mutate into something more permanent, unless there were genuine synergies between the civil businesses of the tank contractors. The prospects for peacetime cooperation were not enhanced by the fact that, unlike the aeroplane, the tank had no commercial uses. There were no commercial spin-offs from the tank programme, except in the narrow area of caterpillar technology. It is possible that a sense of common purpose among firms would have persisted, if the war had resulted in stalemate, followed by a commercial conflict between Britain and Germany, and a continued high demand for armaments. But this is not what happened.[84]

Significant industrial changes did follow the Great War, but they did nothing to inject a spirit of initiative into the former tank assemblers. During the boom of 1919–20, a wave of speculative mergers swept through British manufacturing. But recession rocked business confidence in the early 1920s, and those firms that had merged found themselves in severe financial difficulties. Several tank assemblers were involved in the postwar merger wave. MCWF was sold to Vickers in 1919. Davenport-Hines correctly describes this merger as a 'classic piece of over-capitalisation'.[85] Neither this nor subsequent manoeuvres had a favourable impact on the performance of the rolling stock industry. The COW merged with the rising electrical engineering firm, Dick, Kerr & Co., of Preston, in 1919, to form English Electric. But all attempts to convert the COW's armaments factories to the manufacture of electrical equipment failed, and these plants were virtually idle by 1922.[86]

Those firms that had survived the post-war boom as separate entities fared no better. North British staggered on in the locomotive trade without any real sense of direction. Its brief role in the tank programme was soon forgotten.[87] Fosters reverted to the manufacture of their traditional products, such as thrashing machines, traction engines, and showmen's road vehicles. Foreign competition and weak demand led to the collapse of this strategy, and, in 1928, Fosters diversified by using their cash reserves to purchase Gwynne's Pumps of Hammersmith. Thereafter Fosters gradually withdrew from the agricultural machinery business.[88] Fosters' abandonment of their core business was an extreme measure, and it is possible that a more balanced approach, including the commercial exploitation of wartime advances in caterpillar technology, would have been a better option. Marshalls did introduce some new products, such as oil-driven tractors and central heating boilers, but these met with no more than partial success.[89] It is remarkable that the British agricultural machinery industry did not develop a heavy caterpillar tractor until after the Second World War, since American producers were able to demonstrate that there was a considerable international market for these machines.[90] The failure of Fosters and Marshalls to recognize this rare opportunity to capitalize on their tank work stands as a damning indictment on their strategies.

Many of the wartime producers of tank engines, gearing, and other components were more fortunate than the tank assemblers in the 1920s and 1930s. Gardners went from strength to strength, and became leaders in the design and manufacture of diesel engines for buses. Wrigleys were taken over by Nuffield, and became an important part of William Morris's empire in the motor industry.[91] But it would be rash to claim that their role in wartime tank production accounted for their subsequent achievements. The tank programme was largely self-contained, and it had few long term ramifications for British industry.

5

The Great War was a watershed for many of the older branches of British mechanical engineering. Firms in such sectors as the manufacture of locomotives, rolling stock, and agricultural machinery hoped that the 1920s would witness a return to the solid, if unspectacular, prosperity of the prewar decades. That this did not happen was due to unfavourable market conditions, the growth of foreign competition, and the challenge of rival technologies, such as motor transport. Viewing these trends retrospectively, it seems that diversification would have been the best long term strategy for most of the firms in the older branches of mechanical engineering. Their participation in the munitions effort had provided many of them with experience in the manufacture of unfamiliar products. New skills had been learned, and new contacts had been made with firms in different branches of the engineering sector. The war had shaken British firms out of their old routines. But their war experiences gave companies little guidance about how to achieve equally spectacular results in peacetime. The initiative for industrial diversification, between 1914 and 1918, had come from the government, and the companies that were involved in war production did not have to worry about how to sell their new products. After 1918, however, any further innovation and diversification had to be at the initiative of private industry, and, in consequence, these strategies were rendered far more risky. Perhaps there were few lasting lessons to be learned from the war.

The story of tank production during the Great War provides a clear illustration of the previous points. Like many other munitions, tanks had no commercial applications. Thus, although a complex network of firms was created in order to maximize the output of tanks, there was little prospect that the participants would be able to utilize their experiences and contacts to develop their businesses after the war.

It would be anachronistic to view the industrial war effort solely, or even principally, from the perspective of its long term lessons for British business. Judged on its own terms, the tank complex was a highly specialized network, created by the government, for the maximization of war production. The flexibility demonstrated by the British engineering industry, between 1915 and 1918, was achieved under unusual circumstances, and it was not necessarily a good indicator of what would be feasible under normal peacetime conditions. What was remarkable about the tank programme was the facility with which the government moulded a large and diverse collection of firms into a coherent production network. Previous neglect of the tank programme by economic historians must owe something to the fact that the war ended before the tanks had an opportunity to make their full contribution to the fighting.

Notes

1 I would like to thank John Armstrong, Gordon Boyce, Peter Cozens, Gary Hawke, John King, Michael Miller, Tim Mulcare, and John Wilson for constructive comments on earlier drafts. They bear no responsibility for the results. The Victoria University of Wellington assisted with research expenses.

2 J. P. Harris, *Men, Ideas and Tanks: British Military Thought and Armoured Forces, 1903–1939* (Manchester, 1995), Chs 1–5; T. Travers, 'Could the Tanks of 1918 have been War-Winners for the British Expeditionary Force?', *Journal of Contemporary History*, vol. 27 (1992), pp. 389–406.

3 For a regional study of warships, see H. Peebles, *Warshipbuilding on the Clyde: Naval Orders and the Prosperity of the Clyde Shipbuilding Industry, 1889–1939* (Edinburgh, 1987). There is also a largely political account of the early operations of the Ministry of Munitions: R. J. Q. Adams, *Arms and the Wizard: Lloyd George and the Ministry of Munitions, 1915–1916* (College Station, 1978). But there is no modern analysis of the production of such weapons as guns, shells, small arms, aeroplanes, and poison gas.

4 Each type of tank was divided into male (carrying small artillery pieces as well as machine guns) and female (carrying machine guns alone) varieties.

5 In practice the medium tanks were too slow to keep up with the cavalry.

6 Public Record Office (hereafter PRO), MUN4/2801, Moore to Duckham, 27 Feb. 1918.

7 *History of the Ministry of Munitions* (London, 1921), vol. II, part I, pp. 75, 77.

8 T. Travers, *How the War Was Won: Command and Technology in the British Army on the Western Front, 1917–1918* (London, 1992).

9 Thus tank warfare was more capital intensive than infantry warfare. It should be pointed out that large amounts of infantry were still required. For the classic paper on the economies achieved by tanks on the battlefield, see PRO, MUN4/4979, J. F. Fuller, 'Notes on Tank Economies', 25 July 1918. Edgerton argues that Britain has opted for capital intensive warfare throughout the twentieth century, due to a comparative shortage of manpower, and public sensitivity to high casualties. D. E. H. Edgerton, 'Liberal Militarism and the British State', *New Left Review*, No. 185 (1991), pp. 138–69.

10 For convenience MWD is used throughout this article.

11 Ford assembled Model Ts at Trafford Park. *History of the Ministry of Munitions*, vol. XII, part III, pp. 31, 55, 67; A. G. Wilson, *Walter Wilson: Portrait of an Inventor* (London, 1986), p. 47; D. Burgess-Wiss, 'Lee Dewhurst Perry Percival', in D. J. Jeremy (ed.), *Dictionary of Business Biography*, vol. IV (London, 1985), pp. 639–43.

12 *History of the Ministry of Munitions*, vol. IX, part I, p. 60.

13 PRO, CAB40/2, War Priorities Committee, Minutes of Ninth Meeting, 4 Jan. 1918; MUN4/2801, Minutes of a Meeting held at 10, Downing Street, on March 8, 1918 to Consider the Question of the Output of Tanks.

14 PRO, MUN4/3325, Haig to Secretary of the War Office, 11 Feb. 1917.

15 The Ricardo engine employed in the heavy tank programme was a variant of a design for the Royal Naval Air Service. Medium tanks used the Tylor engine, which was also used in lorries. PRO, MUN5/210/1940/10, Notes on Meeting on Tanks held in Minister's Room on 6 Feb. 1917.

16 PRO, MUN5/211/1940/37, Minute on Engine Position, 10 Aug. 1917.

17 In October 1918, the priorities of the War Cabinet were as follows: first shells, secondly tanks, thirdly the new 18-pder gun, and fourthly aero-engines. This belated emphasis on tanks was a reaction to delays in the construction of the Anglo-American tank factory in France, and to the failure of the Americans to supply tank engines. It did not signify an underlying shift in preferences for tanks relative to aeroplanes. PRO, MUN4/4979, Minutes of the Tenth General Conference of the Controllers of the Warfare Group, 8 Oct. 1918.

18 K. Grieves, *The Politics of Manpower, 1914–18* (Manchester, 1988).

19 PRO, MUN4/5204, Note on Man Hours, 2 Oct. 1918.

20 PRO, MUN5/210/1940/10, Cubitt to Secretary of Ministry of Munitions, 8 Jan. 1916.

21 PRO, MUN4/5204, List of Labour Requirements of Tank Producers, 11 Oct 1918. This document is particularly useful for identifying the main firms engaged in tank production.

22 *History of the Ministry of Munitions*, vol. XII, part III, p. 78.

23 S. B. Saul, 'The Market and the Development of the Mechanical Engineering Industries in Britain, 1860–1914', *Economic History Review*, vol. 20, no. 1 (1967), pp. 111–30; R. Floud, *The British Machine Tool Industry, 1850–1914* (Cambridge, 1976); I. C. R. Byatt, *The British Electrical Industry 1875–1914* (Oxford, 1979); T. R. Gourvish, 'Mechanical Engineering', in N. K. Buxton and D. H. Aldcroft (eds), *British Industry Between the Wars* (London, 1979), pp. 129–55; R. Kirk and C. Simmons, 'Engineering and the Great War: A Case Study of the Lancashire Cotton Spinning Machine Industry', *World Development*, vol. 9, no. 8 (1981), pp. 773–91; J. Wilson, 'A Strategy of Expansion and Combination: Dick, Kerr & Co., 1897– 1914', *Business History*, vol. 27, No. 1 (1985), pp. 26–41; M. W. Kirby, 'Product Proliferation in the British Locomotive Building Industry, 1850–1914: An Engineer's Paradise?', *Business History*, vol. 30, no. 3 (1988), pp. 287–305; J. Singleton, 'Full Steam Ahead? The British Arms Industry and the Market for Warships, 1850–1914', in J. Brown and M. B. Rose (eds), *Entrepreneurship, Networks and Modern Business* (Manchester, 1993), pp. 229–58; J. Foreman-Peck, S. Bowden and A. McKinlay, *The British Motor Industry* (Manchester, 1995), Chs 1–3; P. Dewey, 'The British Agricultural Machinery Industry, 1914–1939', *Agricultural History*, vol. 69, No. 2 (1995), pp. 298–313.

24 S. Pollard, *The Development of the British Economy 1914–1990* (London, 1992), pp. 19–23. This interpretation has its origins in G. A. B. Dewar, *The Munitions Feat* (London, 1921).

25 Experiments had determined that caterpillar tracks were more suitable than wheels for crossing no-man's land, and that a self-propelled vehicle would be more effective than a tractor pulling a battle wagon. *History of the Ministry of Munitions*, vol. XII, part III, pp. 1–31.

26 N. Wright, 'The Varied Fortunes of Manufacturing Industry 1914–1987', in D. R. Mills (ed.), *Twentieth Century Lincolnshire* (Lincoln, 1989), pp. 74–80.

27 *History of the Ministry of Munitions*, vol. XII, Part III, p. 32. The story of MCWF during the Great War is told in R. P. T. Davenport-Hines, *Dudley Docker* (Cambridge, 1984), Ch. 5. This work makes little mention of tanks.

28 *History of the Ministry of Munitions*, vol. XII, Part III, p. 46

29 *Ibid.*, p. 49.

30 PRO, MUN4/2801, Gun Equipment for the Tank Programme, 17 Jan. 1918; MUN4/2797, File 5, Latey to Maddock, 2 Jan. 1919.

31 PRO, MUN4/4979, Tank Supply Department Report, 28 Feb. 1916.
32 PRO, MUN3/83, MCWF to Director Tank Supply Department, 13 Oct. 1916.
33 PRO, MUN5/211/1940/37, Minutes of Conference on Tanks, 11 Feb. 1918.
34 *History of the Ministry of Munitions*, vol. XII, Part III, pp. 33, 42, 43. I have been unable to master the intricacies of engine design.
35 PRO, MUN4/2801, Supply of Engines for Tanks, 28 Aug. 1917; MUN4/4979, Ricardo Engine Production, 14 Oct. 1918; MUN4/5209, Church to Controller MWD, Nov. 1918.
36 PRO, MUN4/2801, Supply of Engines for Tanks, 28 Aug. 1917; A. Muir, *The History of Baker Perkins* (Cambridge, 1968), p. 63. This company was called Werner, Pfeiderer & Perkins until 1915.
37 PRO, MUN5/21/1940/37, Report of Tank Production for Week Ending 27 April 1918; MUN4/5200, Minutes of Scottish Tank Committee, 28 Oct. 1918; MUN4/5204, Mather & Platt to Controller MWD, 10 Oct. 1918; MUN4/4979, Minutes of the Fourth General Conference of the Controllers of the Warfare Group, 29 July 1918; MUN4/5204, Cowley to Controller MWD, 19 Nov. 1918; MUN4/5198, Johnson to Controller MWD, 7 March 1919.
38 *History of the Ministry of Munitions*, vol. IX, Part I, p. 68; B. H. Tripp, *Renold Chains: A History of the Company and the Rise of the Precision Chain industry 1879–1955* (London, 1956), p. 114; G. Tweedale, *Steel City: Entrepreneurship, Strategy, and Technology in Sheffield, 1743–1993* (Oxford, 1995), p. 192; PRO, MUN4/5209, Robert Hyde & Son to Controller MWD, 22 Nov. 1918; MUN4/5204, Bannatyne to Shepherd, 14 Sept. 1918.
39 PRO, MUN4/4979, Minutes of the Tenth General Conference of the Controllers of the Warfare Group on 8 Oct. 1918.
40 *History of the Ministry of Munitions*, vol. VIII, Part III, pp. 72–91; PRO, MUN4/2801, Fleming to Page, 12 July 1917; MUN5/387/1700/6, Memorandum on the History and Work of the Ball Bearing Supplies Department 1916–18, undated [1919–20].
41 PRO, MUN5/211/1940/37, Minutes of Meeting held with Tank Contractors, 20 June 1918.
42 PRO, MUN4/5198, Brown to Controller MWD, 21 Oct 1918; MUN4/5204, West to Controller MWD, 22 Oct. 1918; MUN4/2791, MWSD Inspector, Glasgow to MWSD, 8 March 1917.
43 Tanks were fitted with electric fans in a vain attempt to make their internal temperature bearable. Heat exhaustion was a major cause of incapacity among crews. PRO, MUN5/210/1940/10, Phipps to Secretary of War Office, 2 May 1916.
44 D. Whitehead, *Gardners of Patricroft 1868–1968* (Place of publication unknown, 1968); PRO, MUN4/5209, Church to Controller MWD, Nov. 1918.
45 Thought was given to assembling tanks in Ireland, although this came to nothing. *History of the Ministry of Munitions*, vol. XII, Part III, p. 46.
46 There was a division of labour among tanks. As well as fighting tanks, there were supply tanks to carry supplies or personnel, and gun carriers to carry guns. At the end of the war several tanks were fitted with wireless sets. PRO, MUN5/211/1940/37, Memorandum on 1918 Programme, 4 Sept 1917; MUN4/2801, Memorandum on 1918 Tanks Programme, 26 Nov. 1917. *History of the Ministry of Munitions*, vol. XII, Part III, p. 73.
47 PRO, MUN5/211/1940/37, Minutes of Co-ordinating Committee meeting, 21 March 1918.

48 Patent Shaft & Axletree was a subsidiary of MCWF. PRO, MUN5/211/1940/40, List of Contractors Manufacturing Tanks, 5 June 1918.

49 Scotland's emerging role in the tank programme was cut short by the Armistice. By the start of December 1918 North British had delivered a mere 50 tanks. PRO, MUN4/5200, Minutes of Scottish Tank Committee, 3 Dec. 1918.

50 Dispersal of industry to limit damage from air attack was not necessary during the Great War. Zeppelin raids were no more than a nuisance.

51 No evidence has been found of a regional committee in Birmingham or Lincoln.

52 *History of the Ministry of Munitions*, vol. XII, Part III, pp. 46, 63–5. The role of West's Gas Improvement Company is intriguing. Lord Aberconway remarks that this firm was a force in the gas engineering industry, and that its 'ramifications' were 'world-wide'. The chairman was Lord Mayor of Manchester in the 1920s. Lord Aberconway, *The Basic Industries of Great Britain* (London, 1927), pp. 142–3.

53 For instance, at one meeting of the Scottish Tank Committee, the machining of armour plates, and difficulties with the supply of engines and drivers' hoods, were discussed. PRO, MUN4/5200, Minutes of Scottish Tank Committee, 28 Oct. 1918.

54 PRO, MUN4/5200, Minutes of Scottish Tank Committee, 28 Oct. 1918; *History of the Ministry of Munitions*, vol. IX, Part I, p. 63.

55 It was hard to destroy tanks, but they were easily disabled for a few days. The tracks were particularly vulnerable. *History of the Ministry of Munitions*, vol. XII, Part III, pp. 34, 37.

56 PRO, MUN4/2801, Moore to Duckham, 27 Feb. 1918.

57 E. Devons, *Planning in Practice: Essays on Aeroplane Production in Wartime* (Cambridge, 1950).

58 PRO, MUN4/2801, Capper to Secretary of War Office, 25 Aug. 1917; Cubitt to Secretary of Ministry of Munitions, 30 Aug. 1917; MUN5/211/1940/37, Note by Stern, 24 Aug 1917; Tank Programme, Minutes of Conference held at the Ministry of Munitions, 29 Sept. 1917; *History of the Ministry of Munitions*, vol. XII, Part III, pp. 53, 55, 60.

59 PRO, MUN4/2801, Layton to Secretary of War Office, 26 Jan. 1918.

60 PRO, MUN4/2801, Moore to Director General of Tank Corps, 1 Jan. 1918; MUN5/211/1940/37, Conference on Tanks at Armament Buildings, 11 Feb. 1918.

61 PRO, MUN4/5200, Lobnitz to Churchill, 8 Oct. 1918; Lobnitz to Maclean, 18 Oct. 1918; Minutes of Scottish Tank Committee, 28 Oct. 1918.

62 Beardmores' war is described in M. S. Moss and J. R. Hume, *History of William Beardmore & Co., 1837–1977* (London, 1979).

63 *History of the Ministry of Munitions*, vol. XII, Part III, pp. 49–50, 66; PRO, MUN4/2801, Possibility of Tank Production in 1918, 13 Dec,. 1917; Stallybrass to Hazel, 27 Feb. 1918; MUN5/211/1940/37, Conference on Tanks at Armament Buildings, 11 Feb. 1918; Minutes of Council Committee 57 on Tanks, 27 Feb. 1918.

64 Wrigleys were among the most efficient suppliers of tank gearboxes, and they experimented with flow production. Foreman-Peck, Bowden, and McKinlay, *The British Motor Industry*, p. 37; R. Church, 'Deconstructing Nuffield: The Evolution of Managerial Culture in the British Motor Industry', *Economic History Review*, vol. 49, No. 3 (1996), p. 570.

65 *History of the Ministry of Munitions*, vol. XII, Part III, pp. 60–1, 75; PRO, MUN4/4979, Minutes of the First General Council of the Controllers of the

Warfare Group, 1 July 1918; Minutes of the Second General Council of the Controllers of the Warfare Group, 8 July 1918; MUN5/211/1940/37, Minutes of Meeting held with Tank Contractors, 20 June 1918; Minutes of Meeting of Council Committee on the Production of Tanks, 1 Aug. 1918.

66 PRO, MUN5/211/1940/37, Minutes of Meeting held with Tank Contractors, 20 June 1918.

67 *History of the Ministry of Munitions*, vol. XII, Part III, pp. 37–8, 42–3, 9, 62, 66; PRO, MUN4/5200, Minutes of Scottish Tank Committee, 28 Oct. 1918.

68 The late delivery of drawings was a constant hindrance to the assemblers. PRO, MUN5/211/1940/37, Memorandum on 1918 Programme, 4 Sept. 1917.

69 PRO, MUN4/5204, Lloyd to Maclean, 9 Oct. 1918.

70 PRO, MUN4/4979, Minutes of the Ninth General Conference of the Controllers of the Warfare Group, 1 Oct. 1918.

71 PRO, MUN5/211/1940/37, Minutes of Meeting held with Tank Contractors, 20 June 1918.

72 PRO, MUN4/2791, Taylor to Kellaway, 27 Feb. 1917.

73 PRO, MUN4/4979, Minutes of the First General Council of the Controllers of the Warfare Group, 1 July 1918; MUN4/5204, Crossley Brothers to Maclean, 9 Oct. 1918; Buckmaster to Irving, 15 Oct. 1918.

74 Whitehead, *Gardners*, p. 22. The generally good state of labour relations in the Lancashire engineering industry during the war is discussed in A. J. McIvor, *Organised Capital: Employers' Associations and Industrial Relations in Northern England, 1880–1939* (Cambridge, 1996), pp. 150–8.

75 PRO, MUN5/211/1940/37, Report of Tank Production for the Week Ending 27 April 1918; Moore to Churchill, 4 May 1918. On Armstrong Whitworth during the war, see K. Warren, *Armstrongs of Elswick* (Basingstoke, 1989), Ch. 22.

76 Wright, 'Varied Fortunes', pp. 79–80.

77 As well as taking over the operation of French and Belgian lines for many miles behind the front, the British built new branches and light railways. Traffic was heavy. A. M. Henniker, *Transportation on the Western Front, 1914–1918*, vol. 1 (London, 1937).

78 PRO, MUN4/2790, Moir to Page, 9 Aug. 1917; MUN4/2791, Moir to Duckham, 15 Oct. 1917; Minute by Thomas, 18 Oct. 1917; MUN5/211/1940/37, Memorandum on 1918 programme, 4 Sept. 1918; Minutes of Council Committee 57 on Tanks, 25 Feb. 1918.

79 *Report of the Departmental Committee Appointed by the Board of Trade to Consider the Position of the Engineering Trades After the War.* PP 1918, vol. XIII, p. 10.

80 Alford echoes this conclusion with respect to British industry as a whole: 'the concentrated impact of the war was, potentially, a most effective means of breaking the narrow and limited expectations of businessmen'. This potential was rarely fulfilled. B. W. E. Alford, 'Lost Opportunities: British Business and Businessmen during the Great War', in N. McKendrick and R. B. Outhwaite (eds), *Business Life and Public Policy* (Cambridge, 1986), p. 208.

81 A. D. Chandler, *Scale and Scope* (Cambridge, Mass., 1990), pp. 455–63.

82 Most business leaders were motivated both by self-interest and patriotism. J. S. Boswell and B. R. Johns, 'Patriots or Profiteers? British Businessmen and the First World War', *Journal of European Economic History*, vol. 11 (1982), pp. 423–45. Docker's exaggerated patriotism had its limits. He ordered a go-slow in

tank production during a dispute over prices in 1917. Davenport-Hines, *Dudley Docker*, pp. 100–1.

83 MUN4/4979, Minutes of the Second General Conference of the Controllers of the Warfare Group, July 8th 1918.

84 It was feared, in 1917–18, that the war was tending towards such an outcome. M. W. Kirby and M. B. Rose, 'Productivity and Competitive Failure: British Government Policy and Industry, 1914–19', in G. Jones and M. W. Kirby, eds, *Competitiveness and the State* (Manchester, 1991), pp. 20–39.

85 Davenport-Hines, *Dudley Docker*, p. 165.

86 R. Jones and O. Marriott, *Anatomy of a Merger: A History of G. E. C., A. E. I., and English Electric* (London, 1970), pp. 129–31.

87 R. H. Campbell, 'The North British Locomotive Company Between the Wars', *Business History*, vol. 20, No. 2 (1978), pp. 201–34.

88 Wright, 'Varied Fortunes', p. 82; Dewey, 'British Agricultural Machinery', pp. 307–8.

89 Wright, 'Varied Fortunes', p. 83.

90 Political and Economic Planning, *Agricultural Machinery* (London, 1949).

91 Whitehead, *Gardners*, p. 27; Church, 'Deconstructing Nuffield', p. 570.

Retrospective

The Tank Producers

John Singleton

'The Tank Producers' was a deliberate attempt to fill a gap in the literature on the munitions effort in the First World War.[1] Firms participating in the tank programme had to adapt and learn rapidly. Although the Ministry of Munitions payed a vital role in coordinating the production of tanks, and of munitions more generally, participating firms were not passive agents of the state. They argued back. Government intervention helped organise industry during wartime, but the tank, unlike the aeroplane, lacked a postwar commercial application, and was a dead end until the next conflict.

Arming the Western Front, by Roger Lloyd-Jones and Merv Lewis, offers the definitive account of the munitions programme in the United Kingdom between 1914 and 1918. Lloyd-Jones and Lewis analyse the sometimes fractious relationships between politicians, bureaucrats and manufacturers in an economy constrained by shortages of labour, skills, shipping, and steel. Tanks are by no means neglected in *Arming the Western Front*, but the authors show that they formed a relatively small part of the vast munitions economy.[2] Elsewhere, Lloyd-Jones and Lewis reconstruct the network of firms involved in munitions production in the Manchester district.[3] The organisational issues investigated by Lloyd-Jones and Lewis overlap with those in 'The Tank Producers'. An overview chapter on 'Technology and Armaments' in the *Cambridge History of the First World War* is also worth consulting.[4]

Military and political historians have shown much interest in the study of arms procurement. They tend to approach the archives with different questions than those asked by business historians: this is less a matter of the type of archive visited – 'The Tank Producers' uses government rather than company records – than of perspective. Relations between governments and firms may be glossed over when the emphasis is placed on political and bureaucratic wrangling. Put another way, military historians focus on the demand rather than the supply side of the market for arms.[5]

DOI: 10.4324/9781003313397-7

A monograph by David J. Childs discusses the First World War tank programme, elaborating on the interplay between the spheres of production and performance in the field.[6] Tentative efforts by France, the UK, and the United States to cooperate in the design and production of tanks in the later stages of the First World War are examined by Elizabeth Greenhalgh. She shows how plans for international cooperation generated additional layers of friction and confusion.[7] An article by Ralf Raths on German tank production draws attention to the obstacles in the way of a successful response to the tank by the Central Powers. Raths explains how the customer, in the form of the German army and War Office, were unable to decide on specifications for a tank. Tanks were a low priority under the Hindenburg programme, and only a small number of machines was produced. Raths touches, albeit briefly, on the firms involved in tank production.[8] The complex story of British tank production in the Second World War is told in a monograph and article by Benjamin Coombs.[9]

Except for a chapter on the Swedish ball bearing industry, the recently published collection entitled *The Impact of the First World War on International Business* steers clear of munitions production, concentrating instead on trade and finance.[10] Setting aside foreign-language literature, Lloyd-Jones and Lewis lead the field in the examination of munitions production between 1914 and 1918 from a business history perspective. There remains plenty of scope for new research in this field.

Notes

1 Although a stand-alone article, 'The Tank Producers' explored themes that recurred in my work between the early 1990s and early 2000s. John Singleton, 'Full Steam Ahead? The British Arms Industry and the Market for Warships in Britain, 1850–1914', in Jonathan Brown and Mary B. Rose (eds.), *Entrepreneurship, Networks and Modern Business* (Manchester, 1993), pp. 229–258; John Singleton, 'Vampires to Skyhawks: Military Aircraft and Frigate Purchases by New Zealand, 1950–70', *Australian Economic History Review*, Vol. 42, No. 2 (2002), pp. 183–203.

2 Roger Lloyd-Jones and M.J. Lewis, *Arming the Western Front: War, Business and the State in Britain 1900–1920* (Abingdon, 2016).

3 Roger Lloyd-Jones and M.J. Lewis, 'Lancashire and the Great War: the Organisation and Supply of Munitions to the Western Front', in J.F. Wilson (ed.), *King Cotton: A Tribute to Douglas A. Farnie* (Lancaster, 2009), pp. 223–46.

4 Frédéric Guelton, 'Technology and Armaments', in Jay Winter (ed.), *The Cambridge History of the First World War*, Vol. II (Cambridge, 2014), pp. 240–65.

5 Donald J. Stoker Jr and Jonathan A. Grant (eds), *Girding for Battle: The Arms Trade in a Global Perspective, 1815–1940* (Westport, CT, 2003); Eugene

88   *John Singleton*

Edward Beiriger, *Churchill, Munitions, and Mechanical Warfare: The Politics of Supply and Strategy* (New York, 1997).

6 David J. Childs, *A Peripheral Weapon: The Production and Employment of British Tanks in the First World War* (Westport, CT, 1999).

7 Elizabeth Greenhalgh, 'Technology Development in Coalition: The Case of the First World War Tank', *International History Review*, Vol. 22, No. 4 (2000), pp. 806–36. See also Elizabeth, 'Errors and Omissions in Franco-British Co-operation Over Munitions Production, 1914–1918', *War in History*, Vol. 14, No. 2 (2007), pp. 179–218.

8 Ralf Raths, 'German Tank Production and Armoured Warfare, 1916-18', *War & Society*, Vol. 30, No. 1 (2011), pp. 24–47. This is a very good article, well worth looking up.

9 Benjamin Coombs, *British Tank Production and the War Economy, 1934–1945* (London, 2013); Benjamin Coombs, 'British Tank Production and the War Economy, 1934–1945: Important Considerations for Industry', *History of Global Arms Transfers*, Vol. 5 (2018), pp. 3–18.

10 Eric Golson and Jason Lennard, 'Swedish Business in the First World War: A Case Study of the Ball Bearings Manufacturer SKF', in Andrew Smith, Kevin D. Tennent, and Simon Mollan (eds), *The Impact of the First World War on International Business* (Abingdon, 2018), chapter 4.

Index

Printed in the United States
by Baker & Taylor Publisher Services